Ahsan Academy of Research
(Springs, South Africa)

Moral and Spiritual Transformation in Islam

(Muhammad Fazlur Rahman Ansari' Lectures in South Africa: Reflections)

Vol. 2

Abdul Kader Choughley

Tawasul International
Centre for Publishing, Research and Dialogue
(Rome)

First Edition 2024
ISBN 9791281473348

Author: Abdul Kader Choughley

Ahsan Academy of Research
(Springs, South Africa)
info@ahsanacademy.co.za
www.ahsanacademy.co.za

SHELVCRAFTTM Shelving | Racking |
Display | Shop Fiting Ph: 012 666 8933
Email: sales@shelvcraft.com Website:
www.shelvcraft.com

Tawasul International
Centre for Publishing, Research and Dialogue, Rome, Italy

CONTENTS

Biographical Sketch 5
Acknowledgements 25
Preface 27

Introduction: Mawlānā Fazlur Rahman Ansari's Lecture Visits in South Africa

Mawlānā Ansari in South Africa: Historical Background 29
Mohammed Makki 29
Mawlānā Abdul Aleem Siddiqui 30
 First Lecture Visit (1970) 31
Lectures in Kwa-Zulu Natal 33
Majālis: Islāhi (Reformatory) Perspectives 38
Lectures in Gauteng 40
Lectures in the Cape 42
Tasawwuf in the Cape: Assessment 46
The Muslim Assembly (Cape Town) 50
Life Patronage Conferred 52
Second Lecture Visit (1972) 54
Muslim Youth Movement Background 54
Early Vision of the MYM 55
MYM Convention: As-Salam 55
Unity in Islam: Message 58
Conclusion 61
Lecture Programmes in South Africa: 1970 62

Part One: Lectures Series in South Africa: 1970 and 1972

The Challenge of the Twentieth Century 65
Knowledge and the Self 68
The Principle of Unity (*Tawhīd*) 72
The Age of Doubt: An Overview 75
The Inner Dimensions of Sunnah 79
Philosophy of the Shahādah 81

Muhammad (pbuh): The Prophet of Allah 84
Surah Fātihah and the Concept of Khalifat Allah 88
The Qur'ānic View of Disunity............ 91
Message to the Muslim Youth 94
Westernised Muslims............ 97
Tasawwuf: Spiritual Pursuit in Islam............ 100
Materialism: a Challenge to World Religions............ 103
Women in Islam............ 106
Discipline in Dhikr............ 108
Salāh (Devotional Prayer) 110
What is Islam 113
Our Concept of Islam............ 116
Attainment of Holiness............ 119
Murid (Initiation) 121
Islamic Value System 123
Problem of Human Dignity 125
Why Religion 127
Islam versus Communism 127
The Sunnah: The Challenge 128
Mawlud al-Nabi 128
The Islamic Spiritual Quest............ 128

Part Two: Historic Lectures Series: an Overview

Muhammad the Prophet of Allah (pbuh) 131
What is Islam 132
The Inner Dimension of the Sunnah 133
Salāh (Devotional Prayer) 134
Why Religion............ 134
Islam versus Communism............135
Tasawwuf: Spiritual Pursuit in Islam 136

Conclusion: Gems from the Lectures of Mawlānā Ansari.......139

Biographical Sketch

Mawlānā Muhammad Fazlur Rahman Ansari: Early Influences

Muhammad Fazlur Rahman Ansari was born on 14th August 1914 in Muzaffar Nagar (UP) India. His father Mawlānā Muhammad Khalil (d. 1943) was considered to be an accomplished scholar with strong sufi leanings. His mother Husn Arā Begum (d. 1955) was noted for her piety, generosity and instilling Islamic values among her children. Thus Mawlānā Ansari was born in a religious environment where learning (*'ilm*) was combined with moral upbringing (*tarbiyah*). These traits found fuller expression in the later years of his intellectual and spiritual career.

Their family traced their lineage to the distinguished Sahā bah, Abu Ayyub Ansari. Among his ancestors was the sufi-scholar, Shaykh Abdullah Ansari of Herat (Afghanistan) whose migration to India during the eleventh century was an epoch-making period for his descendants who assumed important positions in disseminating the message of Islam. Likewise another influential Ansari figure was Mawlānā Karim Buksh who was reputed for his unwavering devotion to the *sunnah* and total absorption in *tasawwuf* practices. More importantly, his contributions towards the reform of Muslim society attested to the Chishti teaching of 'service to mankind.'

Mawlānā Ansari had doting parents under whose pastoral care his education began. At the tender age of four years, four months and four days, this child prodigy commenced his *hifz al-Qur' ān* (memorisation). Among the *ashrāf* (Muslim nobility), the *basmala* or induction ceremony of the Qur'ān learning was a notable social event. It was almost like the rites of passage in fathoming the world of the Qur'ān held in veneration among Muslims. Mawlānā Ansari's hifz ceremony was a remarkable achievement and a source of immeasurable pride for the family. The hifz tradition, a phenomenon steeped in centuries of

Islamic tradition across the Muslim world, also served as a benchmark for a family's religious status.

Mawlānā Ansari's retentive memory was considered a Divine blessing. He commenced his hifz at an extremely early age. Based on family accounts he was able to present the memorised passages without any error. Furthermore his mother, Husn Ara was astonished at her son's remarkable ability to memorise the Qur'ān and recite passages at random without revision. He completed his hifz at a tender age of six years and six months. In 1921 he obtained the certificate of hifz al-Qur'ān from Madrasah Islamiyah, Muzaffar Nagar.

Mawlānā Ansari's acknowledgement of his parents' contribution in shaping his intellectual career is expressed in the following words:

> The deepest debt of gratitude I owe, however, to my beloved parents of revered memory: Muhammad Khalil Ansari and Husn Arā Begum, who, through their noble character and fruitful teachings and loving concern for my well-being, built up the foundations of my personality and sponsored and guided my education at all stages, thereby enabling me to undertake this work (*The Qur'ānic Foundations*).

Madrasah Islamiyah Meerut offered the traditional Dars-i-Nizāmi course which Mawlānā Ansari successfully completed in 1933. He initially enrolled as a part-time student in 1921 at the institution and always stood out as a student of exceptional ability and accomplishment. His versatility enabled him to pursue several courses (in many instances unrelated courses) concurrently and independently. It was his stoic spirit and indomitable determination that spurred him to levels of academic excellence.

Mawlānā Ansari's Intellectual and Spiritual Career: An Overview

The period 1932-3 was a turning point in Mawlānā Ansari's intellectual and spiritual career for the following reasons:

- his first meeting with the roving ambassador of Peace, Mawlānā Abdul Siddiqui
- his enrolment at the prestigious Aligarh Muslim university (AMU)

It was no fortuitous circumstances that he met Mawlānā Siddiqui in 1932. A brilliant scholar at the Meerut College, Mawlānā Ansari enjoyed considerable following among his peers. At the same time, Mawlānā Siddiqui had returned from his tabligh tours and was warmly received at the Makhdum Sāhib mosque. Mawlānā Ansari was introduced to him and a strong bond of love developed between the two and soon he became a regular visitor at Mawlānā Siddiqui's home. The relationship reflected the kindred spirit both shared in regard to their respective Islamic and Western educational backgrounds. Mawlānā Siddiqui was eminently suited to hone Mawlānā Ansari's academic skills to the tabligh mission for which he dedicated his life. Moreover in the company of Mawlānā he developed a maturity of outlook and was inducted into the realms of *tasawwuf.* This unique combination of *ta'lim* (education), tabligh and *tasawwuf* in presenting a holistic presentation of Islam provided Mawlānā Ansari with a renewed vigour to serve the cause of Islam. Under the mentorship of Mawlāna Siddiqui, he unleashed his potential as a scholar of extraordinary merit. Mawlānā Siddiqui entrusted him with the responsibility of replying to some of his correspondence and contributing articles to magazines, etc. His writings were done at the behest of Mawlānā Siddiqui and which largely focused on Islamic missionary journalism and practical missionary work. There was no doubt that he had recognised Mawlānā Ansari's capabilities in the field of tabligh.

The Beacon Light

In 1932 when he was only eighteen years he wrote *The Beacon Light,* a first class missionary book on Islam and much earlier he started writing for Colombo's (Sri Lanka) *Muslim Standard* and Singapore's *Real Islam.* Mawlānā Siddiqui's pressing tabligh engagements did not give him sufficient time to respond to the spate of anti-Islamic literature published by Christian missionaries in Singapore. Polemical works denigrating Islamic teachings and the personality of the Holy Prophet (pbuh) continued unabated and, no doubt, there was an orchestrated campaign to thwart tabligh activities among Muslims. Mawlānā Siddiqui's role was two-pronged: to promote the universal values of Islam in Singapore and create a forum for interfaith discussion.

The Beacon Light, a seminal work of Mawlānā Ansari, was a refutation of the missionary's tirade against Islam. It was Mawlānā Ansari who volunteered to write a monograph in defense of Islamic teachings. In a short period of four hours the monograph was completed and in the words of an international law specialist was a flawless piece of work.

Mawlānā Ansari's academic debut was followed by his initiation into *tasawwuf.* The world of Islamic spirituality opened up before him through his association with Mawlānā Siddiqui. In many respects, Mawlānā Ansari's intellectual horizon was broadened and the spiritual dimensions to his personality raised opportunities for his future tabligh mission. Thus his contributions must be examined in the light of Mawlānā Siddiqui's pioneering role during this period. Two strands of thought, intellectual and spiritual, were woven into the rich tapestry of Mawlānā Ansari's multi-faceted career. Tabligh which blended with spirituality assumed greater importance for Mawlānā Ansari in the distinguished company of Mawlānā Siddiqui. Like his spiritual mentor, Mawlānā Ansari's intellectual horizon broadened at the prestigious institution, Aligarh Muslim University (AMU), which was recognised as the cultural centre of Islam in terms of its exemplary academic ethos.

Mawlānā Ansari at Aligarh Muslim University: 1933-47

Mawlānā Ansari's prolonged stay at AMU (1933-47) may be divided into two phases. The first phase 1932-7 saw his meterioc rise as a student of exceptional ability. His undergraduate studies – BA, BSc and BTh attested to his versatile genius. An eighteen month hiatus (1937-8) inducted him into his first tabligh tour to Singapore. Thereafter, the second phase: 1939-47 brought him into prominence on two levels: his conceptualisation of Islamic Philosophy and Comparative Religion which he would develop in later years at the Aleemiyah Institute and his writing output based on a wide range of contemporary issues. These periods brought him closer to Mawlānā Siddiqui both intellectually and spiritually. There was no doubt that Mawlānā Siddiqui's *faidh* (spiritual blessings) opened up opportunities derived from this companionship. Moreover, Mawlānā Ansari served as Mawlānā Siddiqui's private secretary, a position which he held until the latter's death in 1954.

Mawlānā Ansari joined the seat of Muslim learning and culture at AMU in 1933 and enrolled for the BA course. The subjects included in the curriculum were English Literature, Philosophy, Theology, Arabic and Urdu. He graduated in 1935 with a First Class. It was a remarkable feat for Mawlānā Ansari to pursue two degrees concurrently –BA and BSc for which he received the coveted Gold Medal. Another remarkable achievement enhanced his academic profile when he established a new record in Philosophy for obtaining 98% in Philosophy in the BA examinations. In addition to the prestigious awards, he received the Haqqi Prize for meritorious achievement in Arabic. It must be noted that his undergraduate years were a preparatory period for his greater accomplishments in later years at the institution.

In the meantime, Mawlānā Ansari had been pursuing a post Dars-i-Nizāmi course, Bachelor of Theology under the eminent scholar, Professor Sayyid Sulayman Ashraf (d. 1939) who was appointed lecturer in 1902 and later served as chairman, Department of Muslim Theology.

Mawlānā Ansari studied Qur'ānic tafsir and the vast corpus of hadith literature, 'Ilm al-Kalām (scholastic theology) and *tasawwuf* under Sayyid Sulayman Ashraf. He paid glowing tribute to his teacher from whom he acquired knowledge of the Qur'ān and Islamic theological sciences.

Three important points emerge from Mawlānā Ansari's association with Sayyid Sulayman Ashraf. Firstly, as a student he was able to master both classical and literary texts at an advanced level. Secondly, the degree he pursued was equivalent to a specialised study in Qur'ān and hadith.

This required a comprehensive and methodological study of the primary sources of Islam. His profound understanding of these sources are reflected in his writings with particular reference to his major work, *The Qur'ānic Foundations and Structure of Muslim Society*. Lastly, as a celebrated sufi, Sayyid Sulayman Ashraf complemented, by his personal example, the fusion of shari'ah and *tasawwuf*. Like Mawlānā Siddiqui's mentorship in the path of *tasawwuf*, Sayyid Sulayman's teachings about the rich repertoire of classical sufi texts had a definite impact on Mawlānā Ansari.

After Mawlānā Ansari's graduation, Sayyid Sulayman Ashraf had an occasion to make the following remark:

> Hafiz Fazl-ur-Rahman Ansari is a young man with a personality radiant with virtue and exceptional intelligence. As regards his academic distinctions, he holds a place of pride among the alumni of the Muslim University. He has studied the Islamic theological sciences for the most part under me, and has accomplished the task with industry and ability. In *tasawwuf* and philosophy too, he possesses an extraordinary interest and has studied certain classics in both the subjects from me. Islamic missionary work is his goal in life and I pray that Allah Almighty may bestow the choicest success on his labours in that

field.

A similar sentiment was echoed by Professor Abdul Aziz Memon, Chairman, Department of Arabic concerning Mawlānā Ansari's versatility. He commented:

> I have not seen anyone who can equal him in gentleness of manners, excellence of character, love for knowledge, profoundness of concern for the important Islamic problems and courage for shouldering great tasks.
>
> Moreover, in spite of his young age, he does not stand below any seasoned elder in experience and executive ability.
>
> In short, I consider him capable of every good and great pursuit and fit to prove himself equal to any grand task that might be entrusted to him. *Hardly I have seen any student at this University who could excel or even equal him in his attainments which seldom combine in a single person.*

Like many intellectuals at AMU, Mawlānā Ansari's admiration for Iqbal was on account of his contributions to Islamic philosophy. His poems were soul-stirring; his critique of Western civilisation was rigorous and the message for the Muslim *ummah* was optimistic. Moreover, Iqbal had studied in Cambridge and Germany and his writings were enriched by his stay in Europe. His iconic status for students in India could thus not be ignored in their personal quest to study abroad. Mawlānā Ansari's inspiration from Iqbal in this regard was quite understandable. In a letter dated 1937, Mawlānā Ansari sought advice from Iqbal about his intentions to pursue higher Islamic studies in Europe. Iqbal replied:

> As far as Islamic studies are concerned, lecturers at the universities of France, Germany, England and Italy conceal their specific

agendas under the guise of academic research and objective studies. Under these circumstances and keeping your noble intentions in mind, I state without hesitation that your study in Germany will be futile. Instead, go to Cairo (Egypt) and master the Arabic language. Study the Islamic culture, political history, *tasawwuf*, *fiqh* and *tafsir* so that you may be able to reach the true spirit of Muhammad (pbuh). Again, if you are endowed with exceptional intelligence (and potential) and you are passionately inclined to serve Islam, then you may set out your goals as you deem appropriate.

Iqbal's advice as mentioned in the letter contributed significantly to Mawlānā Ansari's career.

The extensive reading by Mawlānā Ansari at AMU covered a wide range of subjects. Therefore, it was hardly surprising that he read voraciously during his undergraduate studies. If his *Beacon Light* introduced him as a student of Comparative Religion, his other book *Muhammad The Glory of the Ages* expressed his mastery of the sīrah literature and trends in modern scholarship in the field of Islamic studies.

Viewed in this historical context, Mawlānā Ansari's scholarly contribution to the life and teachings of the Holy Prophet (pbuh) at a comparatively young age of twenty years must be appreciated. His mastery of the original sources in Arabic and critical assessment of Western scholarship enabled him to provide an unembellished account of the Holy Prophet's message to humanity.

Mawlānā Ansari's profound study of the Holy Prophet's sīrah is clearly elaborated in *The Qur'ānic Foundations*. His coherent arguments in refuting the Christian-Jewish campaign of vilification and presenting a biographical sketch of the Holy Prophet (pbuh) based on Western sources illustrate his devotion to the Holy Prophet (pbuh). For more than forty years, Mawlānā Ansari's writings and lectures focused on an unconditional commitment to the Prophet's message derived from the Qur'ān and *sunnah*. References to the Holy Prophet are aimed at establishing a special rapport with his great personality and imbuing a believer with traits that are embodied in the beautiful conduct of the Holy Prophet.

Tabligh Mission in Singapore: 1937-8

It was during the latter part of 1937 that Mawlānā Ansari was deputed on his first tabligh mission by Mawlānā Siddiqui. The rise of evangelist activities in the Far East Asia especially in Malaya Peninsula necessitated the presence of a forceful scholar who could stem the tide of this growing problem among the Muslim masses in this region. In his *Welcome Address* in Singapore, he categorically stated that he came as the ambassador of the intellectual empire of Islam to reinvigorate and reconstruct Muslim intellectual life. In other words, Singapore and by extension the Malay Peninsula required a renaissance of faith in all aspects of their lives. His pertinent remark about Singapore's future Islamic role vis-à-vis the decline of Muslim countries in other parts of the world reflected his sense of optimism. Mawlānā Ansari was ready to assist in raising up a great new edifice of Islamic civilisation among people "who entered the flow of Islam at a time when the Islamic world had lost its initial vitality and was on the way to succumb to the cultural onslaught of the anti-Western civilisation and could not therefore enjoy the opportunity of building up enduring and vigorous national Islamic traditions and culture."

Mawlānā Ansari's tabligh period (1937-8) was productive in Singapore. He actively promoted the collective identity of the Muslims in the region and sought through his writings to resist campaigns that undermined shari'ah provisions in Malaya. In 1938 a Bill meant to establish the supremacy of Islamic Law in Malaya was introduced in the Federal Status Legislature Council. The entire press dominated by non-Muslims launched a scathing attack on the Federated Muslim States (F.M.S)

Mohammedan Offences Bill. Among the press, the powerful *Straits Times of Singapore* led an editorial campaign captioned "Go to Mosque or Go to Prison" which provoked a series of correspondence and articles undermining the proposed Bill.

Mawlānā Ansari wrote a forceful reply in the *Straits Times* to refute the arguments of all the opponents of the Bill. The editor who was instrumental in writing a scathing editorial was deeply impressed by Mawlānā Ansari's rational exposition that he wrote another editorial, seemingly an apology. His tacit endorsement of Mawlānā Ansari's academic credentials was couched in persuasive language: "that subtle and learned logician."

It must be noted that the period under review (1937-8) nurtured Mawlānā Ansari's academic profile: a scholar with a profound understanding of the challenges facing Muslim communities; an *'ālim* who framed and developed educational programmes compatible to the aspirations of the Muslims, and a *muballigh* who complemented pragmatism and Islam's destiny with progressive orthodoxy. In retrospect, Mawlānā Ansari symbolised Islam's unique role as a da'wah-based dīn capable of responding to modern day challenges.

Likewise, the lecture tours by Mawlānā Ansari to South Africa in 1970 and 1972 were a watershed in the history of South African Muslims. His lectures left an indelible impression on South African Muslims by articulating an Islamic worldview for the new generation of modern educated Muslims.

Academic Honours

In 1939 Mawlānā Ansari was selected as Fellow of the Alexander von Humbold Stiftung of Berlin and was to proceed to Germany to pursue his postgraduate studies. However, with the outbreak of the Second World War in 1939, travel facilities to Germany were equally hazardous and disruptive; thus he had to abandon his ambitious plans. He resumed his studies in

Bachelor of Theology and graduated in 1941 with a First Class First.

Again, the period 1941-2 marked a millstone in his intellectual career and pointed out to his remarkable versatility. He took up the MA course in Philosophy and graduated in 1942. His major subjects included Metaphysics, Ethics, Psychology and Islamic Philosophy for which he was required to study the original sources in Arabic and Persian. The pioneering study in Muslim philosophy entitled *History of Muslim Philosophy* examines the growth and development of this discipline and its close association with the sciences, humanities and arts. Thus a comprehensive study of Philosophy in relation to other disciplines entailed a scientific and rigorous approach combined with an extensive examination of Western sources. At the AMU with its enviable record of producing the best minds in these disciplines, Mawlānā Ansari could not have found a suitable place to pursue his long-cherished ambitions. As the President of the Philosophical Society of AMU, he made important contributions as well. His devotion to learning went beyond the formal curriculum programme. On his own he studied an additional MA course in subjects as diverse as Politics, Economics, Law, Comparative Religion and History of Civilisation and Culture. The world- renowned philosopher, Syed Zafar al-Hasan became his supervisor for his doctorate which he commenced in 1942. Mawlānā Ansari's topic *Islamic Moral and Metaphysical Philosophy* was intended to make ground-breaking research in this field. For five years research work was conducted in an extensive manner.

Even before the completion of Mawlānā Ansari's doctoral thesis, Syed Zafar al-Hasan had recorded his impressions in 1945:

> Hafiz Fazlur Rahman MA., BTh. (Alig) has now been known to me intimately for twelve years. He is recognised by his teachers and his fellow students as an exceptional student, head and shoulders above others, always securing a First Class, standing first and often enough scoring

record marks. For some time he has now been working with me on a philosophico-religious theme for his doctorate, which I am sure is going to be a great dissertation.

Hafiz Fazlur Rahman is a very capable man and has had a vast experience of the world. Already he has published a number of books and pamphlets and articles on Islam and Islamic topics which have been greatly appreciated. He is one of the very few really promising young scholars I know of.

In habits and manners Hafiz Fazlur Rahman is a perfect gentleman – who combines in his person true Islamic culture and occidental (Western) learning and I am sure he will, wherever he goes, add lustre to his own self, his teachers and his great alma mater, the Aligarh University.

Mawlānā Ansari's Doctoral Thesis: Challenges and Opportunities

By all accounts Mawlānā Ansari's thesis was to be a pioneering contribution in Islamic philosophy. Moreover, his detailed studies of tafsir together with his immense grasp of classical texts provided him a scholarly edge to develop his understanding of *tafsir* and the Islamic moral and metaphysical philosophy.

Mawlānā Ansari's assiduous study on his doctoral thesis was not without difficulties. The concepts of Islamic moral and metaphysical philosophy were a new terrain in this discipline and entailed wading through a vast corpus of literature in several languages. As there were no previous studies dealing with this topic, the prospect of formulating new approaches became equally daunting. In fact, five years of intensive study indirectly prepared him for his future role as the exponent of the Qur'ānic teachings derived from the multiple levels of philosophy.

When the thesis was completed and submitted to Syed Zafar

al-Hasan for moderation, the latter had left Aligarh for Karachi preceding the establishment of Pakistan; and thus was unable to present it to the relevant persons in the Philosophy department. After Syed Zafar al-Hasan's death in 1949, efforts were made to trace the research manuscript but could not be found among his belongings. Prior to this, the only other copy of Mawlānā Ansari's thesis was destroyed during his migration to Pakistan in November 1947. His entire library was looted and destroyed in Amritsar (Punjab) and shattered all hopes of retrieving the "fruits of years of laborious and painstaking research."

World Tabligh Tours: 1949-69

The epoch-making and historic tabligh journey during 1949-50 and which lasted for fifteen months was uniquely associated to Mawlānā Siddiqui and Mawlānā Ansari. In many respects, the tabligh journey was unprecedented even during the nineteenth and twentieth century. The countries selected had their respective socio-political pecularities and the Muslim communities were exposed to a number of challenges. In fact, the emerging Muslim communities exposed to the predominantly Western cultures had the formidable task of establishing a viable Islamic presence through institutional forms like the mosques and Islamic centres. The crisis of Muslim identity was inevitable if they failed to address concerns that were directly related to Islamic beliefs and teachings.

In sum, the five tabligh tours which spanned over twenty years were undertaken by Mawlānā Ansari to forge solidarity among diverse Muslim communities in far-flung countries across the continents. He also established Islamic outreach programmes for the purpose of articulating the collective Islamic identity in countries he visited. He strongly maintained that the fusion of knowledge and moral training was the Islamic ideal for Muslim communities.

History of the Aleemiyah Institute

Mawlānā Ansari held important positions at higher institutes of learning. For example, he was appointed lecturer at the University of Karachi to teach Comparative Religion, Islamic philosophy and other disciplines during the period 1960 – 64.

In 1964 Mawlānā Ansari took five years leave without pay in order to establish the Aleemiyah Institute. His growing preoccupation with World Federation of Islamic Missions (WFIM) which required extensive travels abroad forced him to resign from the post. It was at the insistence of Professor Ishtiaq Hussain Qureshi, then Vice - Chancellor of the University, that he continued to be associated with the institution as Director of Research studies in the Department of Islamic Studies, a position which he held until his demise in 1974.

Mawlānā Ansari also studied various branches of medicine during his student days at Aligarh. In 1966, in Karachi, he was registered as an authorised practitioner of homeopathy.

The multidimensional personality of Mawlānā Ansari unfolded at three levels: his academic career, tabligh mission and *tasawwuf* responsibilities. These three areas were contributing factors to his fame as an ‘ālim-scholar.

The nucleus of the Islamic Institute was formed when Mawlānā Ansari had introduced short courses on Islamic studies in a modest flat at Sadar, Karachi to foreign students who wished to be enlightened through the medium of English on Islamic culture and civilisation. The courses continued until the Aleemiyah Institute took a formal shape at the Islamic Centre in July 1964. The first batch of students who hailed from Pakistan, East Africa, South Africa, West Indies and South America pursued the fully-fledged courses in Islamic theology and modern thought.

The Aleemiyah Institute owing to its unique educational programme and dynamic approach carved out a niche as a premier institution of learning and attracted considerable interest from many parts of the world. The list of the first batch of graduates is an indication of the diverse backgrounds of

Muslim students who later served the cause of Islam.

Besides the degrees conferred by the Aleemiyah Institute, the students were given all possible facilities to obtain modern degrees at undergraduate/postgraduate levels according to their preferred areas of specialisation from the University of Karachi. It must also be remembered that Mawlānā Ansari's association with the University as lecturer and Director of Research facilitated the accreditation of degrees at his Institute.

Mawlānā Ansari's life was filled with challenges. One such example was his doctorate in Philosophy thesis which he had completed in 1947. The fruits of his labour lost during the Partition years did not deter him from resuming his doctoral programme at University of Karachi. In 1970 he was awarded the PhD degree in Philosophy. His topic was *Islamic Moral Code and its Metaphysical Background.* His thesis was commented by an eminent scholar of Philosophy, Dr Manzoor Ahmad as follows:

> It is indeed a comprehensive account of the Moral Code provided by the Qur'ān, a like of which, to my knowledge has not been formulated with such an extensiveness by anyone in the history of Muslim literature.

Three years later (1973), Mawlānā Ansari would incorporate his extensive years of study on the Islamic Moral Code in *The Qur'ānic Foundations and Structure of Muslim Society.*

Towards Journey's End

Mawlānā Ansari was a diabetic patient. His strenuous world tabligh journeys, public lectures, writing and teaching took a heavy toll on his health. After the completion of *The Qur'ānic Foundations,* his health deteriorated rapidly. It must be remembered that Mawlānā Ansari also started another project concurrently with this work which was to focus on the hadith literature in relation to the teachings of the Qur'ān. This work was a momentous undertaking and Mawlānā Ansari could not make significant progress owing to the frailty of his physical condition. With his health unattended and to a large extent diabetes uncared for, irreversible damage was caused to his kidneys.

It was on Friday 3 May 1974 that he was admitted to the National Institute of cardio-vascular disease suffering from a mild heart attack and oedema of the lungs. On Thursday 30 May the doctors announced that his kidneys were non-functional and not responsive to the treatment. The concentration of urea in his blood shot up to extreme levels. He was therefore brought home where homeopathic treatment was administered. According to Dr Muhammad Ali Shah, his disciple (*murid*) and allopath physician, he had not come across any case in the annals of medical history, where the mental faculties were so active and vibrant despite the severity of ailments Mawlānā Ansari suffered from. He mustered enough courage to give a concise talk to the medical staff on duty regarding Islamic teachings and the spiritual dimensions of Islam.

Mawlānā Ansari's mental alertness and concern for the mission of Islam was attested by his family members and close associates. His daughter said in the last days she saw her father walking slowly up and down the room reciting the poignant verse of the last Emperor of the Mughal dynasty, Bahādur Shah Zafar:

> *(From the giver and taker of life)*
> I sought and obtained a life span of four days.
> Two have gone in longing (or wishing)
> And two in waiting.

As in verse, so in real life, he spent all his life devoted to one single end, one single goal - the mission of Islam.

This verse alluded to the last days of the Mughal Emperor who was sent to exile in Burma (Myanmar) after the War of Independence in India. An accomplished poet, he symbolised the last vestige of the glorious and often turbulent Mughal rule.

Mawlānā Ansari's zeal for the Islam and his mission sustained the last days of his life. His devoted colleague and lecturer at the

Aleemiyah Institute, Mawlānā Sayyid Abdul Hayy Bukhari said:

> Mawlānā Ansari's concern for the ummah and its future was ingrained in his mind and soul. He said: "After all this hard work and life-long research, I have been able to discover certain truths and diagnose the ailments of the Muslim ummah. How I wish that Allah grants me a few years more to work, so that I may put in my little contribution which is the best in me, for the furtherance of the cause of Islam and Muslims."
>
> But Allah willed that he should rest after a life that was full of hardship, trials, tortures and self-sacrifice. Before he was hospitalised, he had given a particular task to some of the members of the teaching staff of the Aleemiyah Institute. When the writer of these lines visited him in the hospital, he lay in a state of swoon. After a short while, he opened his eyes, looked at the writer, there appeared a feeble smile on his lips, and he said. "How is the work progressing?" He was so weak that his voice sounded as if coming from quite afar. When he was told it was progressing in the normal way, he sighed and said: "Tell them that I shall see it when I come back home."

He did come back home, but not to stay, for soon he had to leave for his eternal abode of bliss.

His humility and devotion to his mission were rewarded with an abundance of knowledge, which often was beyond the realm of human comprehension. On his death bed he said to his wife, Amatas - Subuh Sabiha, his life companion:

> I feel as though the world of knowledge has only now been unveiled to me and all my life. I have been a child grasping tentatively for a ray of knowledge here and there.

Mustafa Fazil, Mawlānā Ansari's only son who succeeded Muhammad Ja'far as khalifah of the Qādiriyyah order, provides the following account of his father's last moments:

> It was the early hours of Monday 6th June 1974, when Dr. Ansari was in intense pain and realising that the doctors could not do anything he then said "Ok, It is now time to leave." He asked me to open all the doors and windows of the room and to give him space. His powerful voice echoed with the melody of *Surah Rahmān*, expressing from the core of his heart his gratitude to his Lord. As he approached the end of the surah, his voice started to fade in slower rhythm. During all this time, he raised his right hand umpteen times as if shaking hands. The whole house appeared to be electrified. With his voice gone, one could see his tongue uttering 'Allah, Allah, Allah....' And then the movement stopped – the saintly soul had departed to meet the Owner, the Lord Almighty, the Beneficent, the Merciful.

A multitude of mourners attended Mawlānā Ansari's *jan āzah* (funeral service). There at the eastern gate of the Islamic Centre, North Nazimabad, Karachi, lay the earthly remains of the noble soul that worked tirelessly and heroically for the cause of Islam.

In Pursuit of Excellence

Apart from public lectures, there were also *majālis* (religious sessions) held at the homes of Mawlānā Ansari's hosts:

- Mawlānā Ansari was accommodating to people from different backgrounds and spoke according to their levels. 'Ulama, professionals and common people visited him and there was no formality *(takalluf)* in his interaction with them. He had that charming smile that endeared people to him. He spoke directly, frankly and honestly. Moreover, it was his spirituality (*ruhāniyat*) that drew people closer to him. Never had visitors seen an 'ālim combine academic excellence with spirituality.

- The *majālis* focused on the universal message of Islām and love for humanity, themes that were woven into his worldview - a poignant reference to sufis who embodied this universal message. Mawlānā Ansari's traditional appearance (*hulyā*) concealed his status as an illustrious scholar with a mind and soul that characterised the era of Islam's glorious past. He was a true representative of intellectual trends that gave shape and character to Islamic scholarship.

- Humility was the hallmark of his character. As much as he shunned self-importance he emphasised personal and spiritual growth–the grades of *tazkiyah* that empower a Mu'min (believer) to unleash his potential to be able to achieve the goals of Divine pleasure (*ridā ilāhi*). It was not uncommon to see throngs of visitors who would discuss their personal matters with him only to leave with a smile on their faces.

- Mawlānā Ansari's conversations were based on the Qur'ān, *sunnah*, lives of the *salf al-sālih*. His exposition of *tasawwuf* was forceful and passionate, spirited and charming as well.

- There was no doubt that his 'ibādāt (*tahajjud salāh, dhikr...*) governed his everyday life. It was the early hours of the morning that revealed his profound spiritual communion with Allah. A restless soul his devotional practices (*awrād*) were conducted in seclusion. The hosts were not inconvenienced.

- Mawlānā Ansari's meticulous observance of the *sunnah* was mirrored in his *tahajjud salāh*. No taxing lecture programmes or other commitments for the day could deter him from his devotional practices in the early hours of the morning. The rapport between an 'abd (servant) and the Almighty Allah through *salāh* and *dhikr* are 'triggers for transformation' which sustain the human personality to achieve the spiritual ideal – Divine pleasure. Mawlānā Ansari personified this spiritual ideal.

- His politeness was proverbial. At the meeting held at the University of Natal (UKZN) he spoke for the allotted time and personally received the next speaker (Rev. Hurley) and led him to the podium. Time management was thus rigorously followed.

A pertinent reminder was given to the audience on the fleeting nature of life and the futility of creating dissension (*fitnah*) by the following comparison:

> "This life here is like the stock of an ice-vendor. He buys the ice from the factory and invests a capital in order to obtain a profit. But he gets back only that much of money in accordance with the quantity of ice he is able to sell. That portion that turns into water is lost in the earth and unreclaimable. All that we do out of love for this world, is like the ice that turned into water and is lost in the earth."

References:

Yasien Mohamed, *Islam to the Modern Mind* (Paarl, 2006).
Mahdie Kriel, *Islamic Intellectual Revival of the Modern Mind* (Cape Town, 2011).
Umair Mahmood Siddiqui, *Dr. Fazlur Rahman Ansari: The Ghazali of His Age* (Karachi, 2016).
Abdul Kader Choughley, *Fazlur Rahman Ansari: Life and Thought* (Springs, 2012).

Acknowledgements

Mahdie Kriel has made pioneering contributions in transcribing, compiling and editing lectures and articles of Mawlānā Ansari. He deserves credit for his substantial interest and remarkable devotion to promoting the life and thought of Mawlānā Ansari through his publications. In more than one way, Mahdie has provided collaborative support for my works on Mawlānā Ansari. When I presented my ideas on this proposed work he granted me permission and his dua's. The title of the book was suggested by Mahdie, which encompasses the versatile contributions of the distinguished scholar of the twentieth century.

It has almost been twenty years since the first edition of *Islam to the Modern Mind* edited by Yasien Mohamed appeared in 1999. The study on the eminent scholar, Mawlānā Ansari, was inspired by Anver Essa of Shelvcraft. His profound admiration for this prominent figure in Islamic resurgence culminated in the number of books which he published. Several editions with a print run of ten thousand copies were distributed at no cost to individuals, academics, universities and organisations in many parts of the world. This was a mammoth task which Anver and his family members meticulously carried out.

Another important work *Islamic Intellectual Revival of the Modern Mind* contains articles and lectures which have been compiled and edited by Mahdie Kriel. In fact these two books are the foundational sources of Mawlānā Ansari's significant contribution to contemporary Islamic thought. Two other works commissioned by Anver, *Fazlur Rahman Ansari: Life and Thought* and *Islam: An Introduction by* Abdul Kader Choughley are representative of Ansari's immense fame. The groundswell of interest in all these works can be gauged from the international interest to his Islamic contributions.

South African Muslims had been honoured in the first half of the twentieth century by the presence of the spiritual luminary, Mawlānā Abdul Aleem Siddiqui. His message of moral and spiritual armament was anchored on his tabligh vision. Mawlānā Siddiqui's lectures in 1934 and 1952 were transcribed by Mahdie Kriel and edited by Yasien Mohamed. *The Roving Ambassador of Peace* was widely acclaimed for its lucidity and concise presentation of this great scholar's Islamic learning. Another study *Abdul Aleem Siddiqui and His Mission* by Abdul Kader Choughley focuses on the revered scholar's multidimensional approach to tabligh.

It will be no exaggeration to state that Anver's publishing efforts on Mawlānā Ansari and Mawlānā Siddiqui are unsurpassed. To date, seven books of exceptional scholarly merit have been published and are indispensable reference works on Islamic reformist thought.

Anver has consistently maintained a low-key profile; his unassuming personality and passionate commitment to Islamic studies are his outstanding traits. His ambitious plans to extend the scope of academic research are illustrative of his vision to promoting Islamic scholarship.

May Allah bless his noble initiatives.

PREFACE

Dr Mawlānā Muhammad Fazlur Rahman Ansari (d. 1974) was a distinguished scholar of Islam whose intellectual contributions in the twentieth century were characterised by his mastery of the Islamic sciences (`ulum) combined with a deep understanding of contemporary issues facing the Muslim communities in a global context.

It is to the credit of Mawlānā Ansari that his international *tabligh* travels spanning several decades created a network of Islamic missions and established platforms to present the message of the Qur'ān to the modern mind. His towering personality exuded an aura of spirituality; his profound knowledge covered an array of subjects that were generally beyond the reach of his contemporaries. In a particular sense, his `ālim credentials combined with his brilliant academic record enabled him to reach out to an audience of diverse backgrounds - Muslim and non-Muslim alike.

Mawlānā Ansari is best known for his widely-acclaimed *The Qur'ānic Foundations and Structure of Muslim Society* which is reflective of his excellent grasp of the Qur'anic themes relating to morality. Likewise, his other writings cover fields of philosophy, comparative religions and critique of ideological systems. These were written at Aligarh Muslim University during his post-graduate studies.

Apart from his writings, his series of lectures have held his audience spellbound. In fact, Mawlānā Ansari captivated the audience in his historic visits to South Africa in 1970 and 1972. These lectures were delivered extempore in symposiums, conferences, halls, mosques and at universities. The thrust of these lectures brought out his brilliant mind and deep concern for the *ummah*. Without exaggeration, he rejuvenated the Muslim community to reconnect with the meaning, message and teachings of the Qur'ān and the sunnah of the Holy Prophet (pbuh). Mawlānā Ansari emphasised the importance of unity - a recurrent theme of his lectures - as a starting point for effective *da`wah* in the country. In the same vein, he warned the Muslim community against theological bickering, which was counterproductive to the spirit of unity.

The present work is a simplified version of Mawlānā Ansari's remarkable lectures contained in the seminal works, *Islam to the Modern Mind* and *Islamic Intellectual Revival of the Modern Mind*. It is a modest attempt to capture the essence of these lectures for interested readers seeking to understand Mawlānā Ansari's presentation of contemporary Islamic thought. A selection of his lectures and writings has been annotated in a volume titled *Moral and Spiritual Transformation in Islam.* The second volume bearing the same title is a succinct presentation of his lectures.

A timeline account of Mawlānā Ansari's lecture programme in South Africa is provided to assess his impact on the Muslim community, particularly the youth who were disenchanted with a rigid interpretation of the Islamic mission and teachings. The array of topics covered by him is a synopsis of the moral and spiritual dimensions of contemporary Islamic thought. To this end, Mawlānā Ansari's multifaceted contributions mark a memorable landmark in South African Muslim history.

Every attempt has been made to convey the essential features of the lectures. At the same time, quotations that have a thematic relevance are highlighted from these lectures to maintain the continuity and fluency of the text. It must be remembered that some of the lectures contain a repetition of themes; therefore, relevant extracts have been selected for this purpose. Mawlānā Ansari's translation of the Qur'ānic verses has been retained. It is evident that the translation was intended to convey a specific meaning within the context of his lectures.

Abdul Kader Choughley
Springs, South Africa
30 August 2024

Introduction

Mawlānā Fazlur Rahman Ansari's
Lecture Visits in South Africa

Mawlānā Ansari in South Africa: Historical Background

The historic lecture visits by Mawlānā Fazlur Rahman Ansari to South Africa in 1970 and 1972 were a historic event for South Africa Muslims. His lectures left an indelible impression on South African Muslims for the following reason: "he was a scholar who could combine the traditional Islamic sciences with modern knowledge and articulate the Islamic worldview for the new generation of modern education Muslims."[1]

Mawlānā Ansari's lecture tours in the country were linked to two important figures who contributed significantly to his acquaintance of the Muslim community.

Mohammed Makki

Mohammed Makki (d. 2003), founder of Makki Publications, had an enviable record of a publishing output in the country. He was responsible for publishing Islamic works, and *Ramadan Annual* for 65 years which was well received in South Africa and beyond its borders. After spending several years at an Islamic institution in Meerut under the tutelage of Mawlānā Abdul Aleem Siddiqui, Makki continued his studies at the hands of Mawlānā Siddiqui's equally renowned elder brother, Mawlānā Ahmad Mukhtar Siddiqui. It was in 1934 when Makki brought Mawlānā Siddiqui to visit the country for a series of lectures. In that year, Makki Publications was founded and Mawlānā Siddiqui served as its first patron. Makki was responsible for printing Islamic publications such as 'FivePillars, PakNews, Qadiani Movement' and *The Muslim Digest* and *Ramadan Annual* up to the year 1999.[2]

---

[1] Mohamed, *Islam to the Modern Mind,* (Cape Town, 2006), 20.
[2] Information provided by Adam Kolia, co-editor of *Ramadan Annual* (19 April

Acccording to Shamil Jeppie, these publications "showed a remarkable consistency and Makki produced them since their beginnings on a shoestring budget and without administrative infrastructure."[3] He also spearheaded the campaign against Joseph Perdu, a Bahai missionary who attempted to disseminate his deviant beliefs among the Muslim community.[4]

Mawlānā Abdul Aleem Siddiqui

It was the second lecture visit in 1952 lasting six months that established the prominent personality of Mawlānā Siddiqui in the country. His series of lectures across the country bore the themes of *Unity in Islam* and *Love for the Holy Prophet* (pbuh). The reception accorded to him in Cape Town at the Grand Parade by no less than a 36000 crowd of Muslims[5] was a testimony to his fame in the country. Most of Mawlānā Siddiqui's lectures were delivered in the mosques in Pretoria, Durban and Cape Town. His lectures were recorded by Haji Ebrahim Tarmahomed (d.1997).[6] Moreover, his contributions were not only confined to public lectures but in the establishment of Muslim schools, mosques and also the propagation of Islam among the Black community.[7]

Mawlānā Siddiqui was succeeded by Mawlānā Ansari in 1954 after his death. In that year he became the Patron of the Makki Publications. Makki played a pivotal role in publishing the writings (in particular the insightful articles) of Mawlānā Ansari through his journals. Mawlānā Ansari's monographs[8] dealing with the

---

2012).

[3] Shamil Jeppie, *Language Identity, Modernity, The Arabic Study Circle of Durban* (Cape Town, 2007), 92.

[4] Ibid., 89-94, See Shamil Jeppie, Identity Politics and Public Disputation: A Bahai Missionary as a Muslim modernist in South Africa, in *Journal for Islamic Studies*, Vol. 27, 27: 150-72.

[5] Cited in *The Muslim Digest* Feb/March, 1993, 169.

[6] *The Muslim Digest*, 1998; 340. A eulogy on Haji Ebrahim Tarmahomed appears in the same issue.

[7] Mohamed, *The Roving Ambassador of Peace*, ix-x.

[8] See Ansari, Islam: The Religion of Unity and Progress, in *The Muslim Digest*, July 1961, 3-9. Cf. Ansari, Foundations of Faith, Part xx in *The Muslim Digest*, December 1964, 15-20.

rational exposition of Islam were serialised in *The Muslim Digest.* Likewise, World Federation of Islamic Missions (WFIM) and Aleemiyah Institute of Islamic Studies established by Mawlānā Ansari were also promoted by Makki. No doubt, Mawlānā Ansari's articles enhanced the academic profile of Makki Publications, especially *Ramadan Annual* which otherwise was described as "a yearly miscellany of mostly borrowed articles."[9]

First Lecture Visit (1970)

Mawlānā Ansari's initial planned visit was organised for 1969 but his heavy schedule in respect of his fifth world tabligh travels and preoccupation at the Aleemiyah Institute delayed this historic visit.

Firstly, he arrived on 20 August 1970 at the Louis Botha Airport in Durban and received an enthusiastic welcome where he was presented with garlands by the officials of the numerous Muslim organisations that came. The lectures delivered by Mawlānā Ansari in major towns and cities across the country were considered momentous occasions and reflected his position as a scholar of world renown.

The following report summarises his impact on the Muslim community of South Africa:

> Everywhere in South Africa, ever since the day that he arrived here, Dr Fazlur Rahman Ansari has been accorded the same enthusiastic welcome by the entire Muslim community of this country. All the lectures and talks that he has given have been followed enthusiastically and with the closest interest by all Muslims, both male and female everywhere. For the Muslim youth in South Africa in particular, Dr Ansari has a special appeal because of his outstanding eminence as probably the most educated Muslim scholar of Western repute. The same applies to the

---

[9] Shamil Jeppie, *Language Identity Modernity*, 92.

female section of our community who are very keenly interested in the approach that Dr Ansari makes on the problems that confront Muslim society generally. It is this interest and enthusiasm that is being so markedly shown in the talks and the lectures of Dr Ansari by the Muslim youth particularly, that are so encouraging to us all. They (lectures) demonstrate very clearly indeed the influence that is being made upon the hearts and the minds of young Muslims who do need so sorely guidance in those fields while Dr Ansari is so completely able to provide the required guidance. Even the newspaper "The Daily News" of Durban carried a report on Dr Ansari's impact on the youth by the heading "Islamic Theologian is a big hit with the Youth."[10]

It would be worthwhile to examine the religious and political conditions in the country prior to his visit. According to Farid Sayed, anti-apartheid forces among the Muslim youth were mobilised in order to express solidarity with the dispossessed majority in the country. Marxism was a contending ideology to established religions including Islam and had infiltrated institutions and schools which were a fertile ground for radical views. The Muslim youth were disenchanted with the ritualistic exposition of Islam and therefore embraced Marxism as a viable ideology. It assumed the function of an advocacy group which, inter alia, worked towards a social justice paradigm as opposed to the draconian apartheid legislations.

Mawlānā Ansari's visit to the country was a landmark for several reasons. First, he presented a conceptual framework for promoting Islamic ideals that were perceived to be out of the realms of scholarly discourse. Second, his academic profile deconstructed the stereotypical representation of the ʿulamā cocooned in their rigid domains of conservatism. Third, the fusion of science and religion was elaborated on rational grounds. Last,

---

[10] Report: *Dr Ansari in South Africa* (1970).

he was unambiguous in identifying the malaise affecting the *ummah* and at the same time offering a remedy in context of the realities Muslims faced in the country.[11]

According to Advocate Hafiz Abu Bakr Mahomed, the lectures Mawlānā Ansari delivered during his short visits to the country dealt with three broad themes. They embodied "a deeper understanding of the basic principles of Islam, and Islamic response to the intellectualchallenges of the twentieth century and the methodology of Islamic spirituality."[12]

Lectures in Kwa-Zulu Natal

Following Mawlānā Ansari's impressive reception welcome speech, programmes were organised in Kwa Zulu Natal beginning with Durban. Mohammed Makki and A.G. Khan, trustee of the Juma Mosque, coordinated the lecture programmes.

The lectures on *Islam and Marxism* and *Islam versus Communism*[13] contained a thematic message: ideologies were antithetical to the spirit of Islam. It must be remembered that Mawlānā Ansari's lectures were extempore and he was an ocean of knowledge *(bahr-al ʿulūm)* in his critical examination of ideologies like Marxism and Communism.

What set Mawlānā Ansari apart from the academics and ʿulamā was his mastery over Islamic and secular disciplines. According to Mawlānā Ansari, Marxism and Communism thrived on the notion of materialism and expediency.[14] If Marxism opposed capitalism it advocated materialism as an alternative system operating in a godless culture. Likewise, Communism believed in the dictatorship of the proletariat which actually meant the dictatorship of a select few.[15]

Islam condemned these ideological systems because they deprived mankind of their intrinsic values and highest yearnings,

---

[11] Report: *Dr Ansari in South Africa* (1970).

[12] Interview with Farid Sayed, Editor of *Muslim Views,* Cape Town (22/4/2012).

[13] Review of *Islam to the Modern Mind.* Fourth Edition, 2006.

[14] Mohamed, *Islam to the Modern Mind,* 204-10.

[15] Ibid., 208.

and a moral and spiritual system. Again, the theme of *Khalifāt Allah* (mankind's Divine responsibility) was emphasised.

Mawlānā Ansari's critique of Marxism and Communism must be seen in relation to Muslim leadership which established a political alliance with communist countries in the early 1970s.[16] The consequence was disastrous for both Islam and the ummah. Muslim leadership was a hybrid of de-Islamised and de-culturised elementswith no faith in the dynamic spirit of Islam in all facets of human endeavour.

Likewise, Mawlānā Ansari expressed his candour at the Muslims' inability to resist the challenges of materialism advanced by Marxism. In his insightful lecture *Materialism: A Challenge to World Religions*[17] Mawlānā Ansari reiterated Muslim predicament in the country within the context of his lecture. He said that Muslims needed "a definite, positive and dynamic effort to go back to Allah, back to the higher values as exemplified by the holy personalities that Allah had sent to various communities of mankind." In his estimation, equality of mankind was synonymous with the honour Allah had conferred on the children of Adam. This implied that Muslims should reassess their role in life. A bold step, Mawlānā Ansari contended, was to understand the implication of the callto 'Discover God again.' It involved "a real vibrant, dynamic and living faith in Him."[18] For Ansari, a community inspired by goals reflecting theIslamic principles of goodwill, and selfless love for mankind can confront the "hydra-headed monster of materialism and permissive society."[19]

Mawlānā Ansari's two lectures on the personality of the Holy Prophet (pbuh) also deserve mention. At the Juma Mosque, Durban, he elucidated aspects of the Holy Prophet's (pbuh) personalitythat pointed out to his extraordinary status.[20] He added that through the emulation of the Holy Prophet (pbuh) can true

---

[16] Pakistan's alliance with Russia which also veered towards India for political expediency is one example.

[17] Mohamed, *Islam to the Modern Mind*, 288-94.

[18] Ibid., 291.

[19] Ibid., 291-2.

[20] Report: *Dr Ansari's visit in South Africa* (1970), 1.

love for Allah be established as exemplified in the following Qur'ānic āyah:

O Prophet, proclaim unto Muslims: 'If you love Allah (tie yourself behind me), imitate me all the time.' (3: 31)

Mawlānā Ansari's homage to the Holy Prophet (pbuh) is succintly expressed in these words:

"Thus, a person cannot walk the way of becoming beloved of Allah without becoming a slave of the personality of the Holy Prophet (pbuh)."

Any attempts to diminish the sublime status of the Holy Prophet (pbuh) are a result of a Muslim's flawed understanding of his divine mission. In the final analysis, Muslims are reminded of their own limitations:

"We are pygmies and therefore we wish to measure the Holy Prophet (pbuh) with our dwarfish status."[21]

Mawlānā Ansari's lectures on *Iqbal and the Holy Prophet Muhammad* (pbuh) was an enlightening presentation on the Poet of the East's devotion to Holy Prophet (pbuh). According to Abdullah Deedat, a noted scholar of Iqbāliat, Arabic and an educationist, Mawlānā Ansari's copious references to Iqbal's poetry illustrated the influence of the latter's *Reconstruction of Religious Thought in Islam* on his writings. The Qur'ān, he asserted, was the reference point to a proper understanding of Islamic teachings. Iqbal's ideas of a Muslim, according to Mawlānā Ansari, is linked to the Qur'ānic message - a pivotal community in the world that is the instrument of the Divine Will. In other words, the Muslim community can only assume leadership if it is based on the Qur'ānic message and the Holy Prophet's (pbuh) noble conduct both of which reaffirm the destiny of the Muslim

---

[21] Mohamed , Mawlud al-Nabi, in *Islam to the Modern Mind*, 287.

ummah.[22]

Abdullah Deedat and other leading stalwarts in Durban were responsible for the publication of the periodical, *Al-Mujaddid.* The editorials and articles reminded Muslims to have a direct access to the word of Allah (Qur'ān) rather than the dogmatic interpretationof `ulamā.[23] *Al- Mujaddid* also attempted to promote a contemporary understandingof Islam and invoked names like Sayyid Ahmad Khan, Jamāluddin Afghāni and Iqbal as modern heroes of Islam.

Abdullah Deedat noted that Iqbal's deep-seated and unconditional love for the Holy Prophet (pbuh) was based on *ishq* (passionate love) in its broadest sense. Therefore, an unmediated access to the rich Islamic treasures (*turāth*) needed to be appropriated in order to achieve its maximum potential. The nexus (*nisbat*) of intense love and devotion can only be manifested when there is totalabsorption in emulating the life and personality of the Holy Prophet(pbuh) based on the *fanā fi al-Rasul* ideal.

As Iqbal said:

"Take thyself to the feet of the Holy Prophet (pbuh) for he alone is all religion – the whole religion! If youcannot become a true lover of him then all your prayers and deed taken together makes of you an Abu Lahab and not a Muslim."[24]

Mawlānā Ansari's immense respect for the Holy Prophet's (pbuh) unique status is brought out in these words:

We know that charcoal is pure carbon and diamond is pure carbon. It is only the frequency of the vibration of the molecules thatmakes them different. The Holy Prophet (pbuh) is like a diamond and we are charcoal.[25]

---

[22] See *Al-Islam*, vol. 2, No. 2, October/November 1971.

[23] For a brief overview on *Al-Mujaddid* periodicals, see Jeppie, *Language Identity Modernity*, 95-100.

[24] Mohamed, *Islam to the Modern Mind*, 79.

[25] Ibid., 84.

The diversity of audience in terms of their academic and professional backgrounds prompted Mawlānā Ansari to deliver a lecture on the quest for religious values. At the M.L. Sultan College the topic *Why Religion* highlighted Mawlānā Ansari's fortè in the field of philosophy. His cogent arguments followed by a historical analysis of materialistic philosophy pointed out the inherent flaws of these theories that aimed at undermining the belief in the existence of God. In repudiation of these theories, Mawlānā Ansari boldly stated:

> Islam says that God is Absolute Good and whatever he created is Absolute Good. Consequently, all our activities in this world are good and it becomes really good when every activity is undertaken with the fullest consciousness that a person is behaving as a co-worker with God in His divine scheme. Every activity is for Hissake and not for any ulterior motive.[26]

Mawlānā Ansari's rational presentation of Islam attracted the interest of medical practitioners who raised questions relating to their profession. Among the vexing questions were Darwinism, birth-control and pre-destination. It goes to the credit of Mawlānā Ansari that he was the only `ālim who could provide rational explanation of Islam's view on these contentious topics.[27] Several decades later, a graduate of the Aleemiyah Institute and Temple University (USA), Professor Abul Fadl Mohsin Ebrahim, wrote scholarly works about the Islamic perspective on bio-medical issues.[28]

Mawlānā Ansari's inspiring lectures also drew appreciable interest among non-Muslim professionals. At a multiracial gathering in the Durban City Hall, Mawlānā Ansari held the

---

[26] Bearing the same title *Why Religion* (1996), Mawlānā Ansari's lecturer, S.Z. Hasan has also elucidated these concepts in his monograph. Cf. Mohamed, *Islam to the Modern Mind,* 156.

[27] Report: *Dr Ansari in South Africa,* 2.

[28] See Abul Fadl Ebrahim, *Reproductive Health and Islamic Values, Ethical and Legal Insights* (Durban, 2011).

audience spell- bound when he spoke on *Islam's Contributions to Human Civilisation*. In fact, Mawlānā Ansari elaborated on the salient features of Islamic culture and its impact on world civilisations over the centuries:

> "The Holy Qur'ān came to impart a correct philosophy of culture and beyond that, to lay the foundations of a new civilization. And a new civilisation came into existence – a balanced civilisation conceived in terms of the realisation of Piety, Truth, Wisdom and Service to humanity and based on the concept of integralistic (holistic) culture."[29]

As in his past tabligh travels, arrangements were made to meet state dignitaries so that the message of Islam could be conveyed to them. A meeting was held with Mr. Warman, Mayor of Durban during which Mawlānā Ansari exchanged views on Islam and Christianity and the challenges faced by Abrahamic faiths.

Islam and Marxism appeared to be a crucial topic for students at the Union Hall (KwaZulu-Natal University). However, the lecture indirectly challenged Mawlānā Ansari's academic credentials, who in his flowing robes and sufi attire was perceived to be another traditional `ālim with 'second-hand' knowledge of the ideology. The meeting was presided over by the Archbishop of Durban, Dennis Hurley. Mawlānā Ansari's exposition of the topic dispelled any misgivings about his academic profile.[30] He was an Islamic scholar trained in secular sciences, an original thinker who was rightly called the representative (*tarjumān*) of Islam.

Majālis: Islāhi (Reformatory) Perspectives

Apart from public lectures, there were also *majālis* (religious sessions) held at the homes of Mawlānā Ansari's hosts. Moosa Paruk, a renowned industrialist and host to many `ulamā from South Asia[31] gave his personal reflections of his guest, Mawlānā

[29] Ansari, *The Qur'ānic Foundation*, vol. I, 199-200.
[30] Report: *Dr Ansari in South Africa,*

- Mawlānā Ansari was accommodating to people from different backgrounds and spoke according to their levels. `Ulamā, professionals and common people visited him and there was no formality (*takalluf*) in his interaction with them. He had that charming smile that endeared people to him. He spoke directly, frankly and honestly. Moreover, it was his spirituality (*ruhāniyat*) that drew people closer to him. Never had visitors seen an `ālim combine academic excellence with spirituality.

- The *majālis* focused on the universal message of Islam. *da`wah*, practising Muslims and love for humanity. These were themes that were woven into his worldview - a poignant reference to sufis who embodied this universal message.[31]

- Mawlānā Ansari's traditional appearance (*hulyā*) concealed his status as an illustrious scholar with a mind and soul that characterised the era of Islam's glorious past. He was a true representative of intellectual trends that gave shape and character to Islamic scholarship.

- Humility was the hallmark of his character. As much as he shunned self-importance, he emphasised personal and spiritual growth – the grades of *tazkiyah* that empowered a *mu'min* (believer) to harness his potential in order to achieve the goals of Divine pleasure (*ridā ilāhi*).

- It was common to see throngs of visitors who would discuss their personal matters with him only to leave with a smile on their faces.

- Mawlānā Ansari's conversations were based on the Qur'ān, sunnah, lives of the *salaf al-sālih* (pious precursors). His exposition of *tasawwuf* was forceful and passionate, spirited and charming as well. The lives of distinguished sufis served as a frame of reference for appreciating Islam's rich legacy (*turāth).*

---

[31] Moosa Paruk was responsible for organising several visits of Professor Ahmad Saeed Akbarabadi (d.1984), a noted Islamic scholar, to South Africa.

- There was no doubt that his `ibādāt (tahajjud salāh, dhikr...) governed his everyday life. It was the early hours of the morning that revealed his profound spiritual communion with Allah. A restless soul, his devotional practices (*awrād*) were conducted in seclusion. The hosts were not inconvenienced.
- His politeness was proverbial. At the meeting held at the University of Kwa Zulu-Natal, he spoke for the allotted time and personally received the next speaker (Rev. Hurley) and ledhim to the podium. Time management was thus rigorously followed.[32]

Lectures in Gauteng

Mawlānā Ansari's lecture programmes in Gauteng were held mainly in Pretoria (Tshwane) and Johannesburg. The Pretoria Muslim Youth Brigade was in attendance to welcome Mawlānā Ansari on his arrival in Laudium. Under the auspices of the Pretoria Islamic Society lectures were delivered at the Church Street (Pretoria) and Jewel Street (Laudium) mosques. The topic *The Principle of Unity* was linked to the theme of *Unity of God*.[33]

According to Mawlānā Ansari, the concept of unity is the foundation of the Muslim community and the very essence of Islam. Therefore, the ideals of *ummatan wāhidatan* (one community) and the Divine command are emphasised, which Muslims are expected to carry out faithfully. Negative traits, Mawlānā Ansari lamented have eroded the spirit of brotherhood and unity. Thus, the projection of individual egos assume the forms of self-interest and self-importance that have a debilitating effect on the *ummah*. Moreover, the foundation of unity was built on the sacrifices of the Holy Prophet (pbuh) and his Sahābah. Sadly, Islamic history is replete with tragic incidents which led to the collapse of the Muslim empires in Spain and India during the heydays of their respective rule. Mawlānā Ansari's message is

---

[32] Interview with Moosa Paruk (Durban), 28/01/2012.
[33] Report: *Dr Ansari in South Africa* (1970), 3-4.

clear: *tawhīd* is indivisible; *ittihād* (unity) among Muslims is irreversible.

A pertinent reminder was given to the audience on the fleeting nature of life and the futility of creating dissension (*fitnah*) by the following analogy:

> This life here is like the stock of an ice-vendor. He buys the ice from the factory and invests a capital in order to obtain a profit. But he gets back only that much of money in accordance with the quantity of ice he is able to sell. That portion that turns into water is lost in the earth and unreclaimable. All that we do out of love for this world, is like the ice that turned into water and is lost in the earth."[34]

What is with you must vanish: what is with Allah will endure.

(16: 96)

Several lectures in the form of *wā'az* (religious counsels) were delivered in the Johannesburg mosques as well. Doctrinal differences were set aside during his lectures largely on account of Mawlānā Ansari's impassioned appeal for unity among the Muslim community.

A meeting with professionals of the Aligarh Old Boys Association of South Africa rekindled memories of their alma mater. He was also appraised of the contributions of the Associationin the educational field.

Like in Durban, Mawlānā Ansari's presence in Laudium attracted a number of visitors at the residence of Aboobaker Moosa Kalla, a regular contributor of articles to Makki Publications.[35] Themes of love for Allah, devotion to the Holy Prophet (pbuh) and emulation of the *awliyā-Allah* dominated the discourses of Mawlānā Ansari and nourished the souls of the visitors in these *majālis*.

Mawlānā Ansari's meticulous observance of the sunnah was mirrored in his *tahajjud* salāh. No taxing lecture programmes or other commitments for the day could deter him from his

---

[34] Mohamed, *Islam to the Modern Mind*, 63.
[35] *The Muslim Digest* and *Ramadan Annual.*

devotional practices in the early hours of the morning. The rapport between an ʿabd (servant) and the Almighty Allah through salāh and dhikr are 'triggers for transformation'[36] which sustain the human personality to achieve the spiritual ideal – Divine pleasure. Mawlānā Ansari personified this spiritual ideal.

Lectures in the Cape

Mawlānā Ansari's lecture travels in the Cape had a two-fold mission: to strengthen the Islamic traditions embedded among the Cape Muslims for almost three centuries; and to reinforce *tasawwuf* through the contributions of sufi shaykhs like Shaykh Yusuf of Macasar[37] and other divines who had settled in the Cape in the three centuries and had made a great impact on the inner dimensions of Islam.[38]

In Cape Town Haji Zubair Sayed (d. 1974), founder of the Islamic Research Publications Bureau in 1952 and *The Muslim News* played host to Mawlānā Ansari. The Bureau published the monographs of Mawlānā Siddiqui and Mawlānā Ansari and through its efforts the Muslim public became acquainted with the works of Mawlānā Ansari who up to then had not visited South Africa. A Welcome Reception was held at the Cape Town City Hall where Muslims and non-Muslims assembled in their thousands to listen to Mawlānā Ansari's lecture. It had a huge impact on the audience who came from different professional backgrounds.

Mawlānā Ansari's visits to several high-profile organisations were a tacit endorsement of his prominent status. At the Siddiqui Mosque named after his spiritual guide, Mawlānā Siddiqui, Mawlānā Ansari delivered a lecture entitled *Women in Islam*.[39] His rational presentation of a Muslim woman's role in society did not

---

[36] Ismail Kalla, *Unleashing the Power of the Almighty Allah Within You* (Pretoria, 2011), 123

[37] Suleyman Dangor, *Shaykh Yusuf of Macassar* (Durban, 1994), 54-65.

[38] For a detailed discussion about the influence of *tasawwuf* on Islamic practices in the Cape, see Yusuf da Costa and Achmat Davids (eds), *Pages from Cape Muslim History* (Pietermaritzburg, 1994), 129-42.

[39] Mohamed, *Islam to the Modern Mind*, 211-226.

betray streaks of chauvinism or apologia. Instead, he outlined the social system of Islam which worked within natural laws governed by Divine wisdom. The first principle of Islamic social life stated clearly that men and women should base their lives on goodwill and understanding. Mutual consultation was a prerequisite and ordained by Allah:

Who conduct their affairs by mutual consultation... (42:38)

Mawlānā Ansari emphasised that women formed an integral component of humanity and personified the maxim "the hand that rocks the cradle rules the world." Therefore, it was no fault of Islam when different Muslim communities distorted the role of women in society by adopting extreme measures deemed un-Islamic. Likewise, Mawlānā Ansari refuted the claims of modernists who believed that *purdah* was oppressive and a social vice. In his imitable style, Mawlānā Ansari highlighted the dignified position of women in Islam and how the *purdah* system enhances her status as a diamond that is not meant for prying eyes. In contrast, the position of women in the Western society is a contradiction: ironically, her freedom is exposed to permissiveness which allows men exploit their vulnerability and ruin their dignity. Mawlānā raises a compelling question: can diamonds be equated with pebbles strewn around the streets?

The Azzawiya Mosque founded in 1920 in Walmer Estate was also visited by Mawlānā Ansari. Mawlānā Siddiqui also made frequent visits to this mosque and maintained cordial relations with Shaykh Mahdie Hendricks and Shaykh Ebrahim Hendricks.[40] The topic *Challenges of the Twentieth Century* was a clarion call for Muslims to internalise the universal message of Islam in their lives. Mawlānā Ansari deplored the intellectual, moral and spiritual stagnation affecting the *ummah*. There was a dearth of intellectual geniuses like Imām Ghazāli, Imām Shāfi', Imām Rāzi and many others. The cause could be attributed to a stifling intellectual climatethat failed to reactivate a semblance of the

---

[40] See Mohamed, *The Roving Ambassador of Peace*, 109-110.

Prophetic era.[41] Despite the doom and gloom syndrome which was symptomatic of Muslim life, Mawlānā Ansari urged Muslims to follow the Prophetic model(*uswah-al-hasanah*). He said:

> Even if one spark remains, it can be converted into the biggest fire that can burn out all the evil within us. This is the same spark our Holy Prophet (pbuh) placed in the hearts of his Companions. This spark is that genuine *imān* in Almighty Allah. If we can only understand that *imān* is not a mere ritual or formal exercise, but something real and alive which must be cultivated. This force made our forefathers great and this *imān* became the real challenge. But this *imān* was not for any racial or political aggrandisement, nor for causing any harm or evil to anyone. This *imān* was a challenge only for the establishment for all that is good and eradicating all that is evil for all humanity.[42]

A series of lectures was delivered at University of Cape Town. A symposium was organised by the University of Cape Town Islamic Association. The topic was *Do the Different Religion of World offer a Solution to the Problems of the Twentieth Century?* Speakers besides Mawlānā Ansari were Professor Cumpsty, Head of the Department of Religious Studies and the Chief Rabbi of Cape Town.[43] Mawlānā Ansari's vast learning and depth of study of comparative religion was recognised. His logical presentation and coherent reasoning were outstanding traits that characterised the tone and tenor of his lecture on comparative religions. The absence of polemics which otherwise tends to mar an objective analysis of dogmas and beliefs of Abrahamic faiths was a marked feature of his exposition of Islam as a world and final religion.[44]

Three strands of thought were woven into Mawlānā Ansari's

---

41 Ansari has elaborated the theme of Muslim decline from a historical and political perspective in his major writings.

[42] Mohamed, *Islam to the Modern Mind*, 148.

[43] Report: *Dr Ansari in South Africa*, 4.

[44] Interview with Farid Sayed. (21/04/2012).

lectures at the University of Cape Town. First, unity of mankind, knowledge and nature presupposes man's role as *Khalifat Allah*. The Qur'ān in numerous *āyāt* (verses) sets out clearly the principle of unity in the natural phenomena. Islam encouraged the inductive method of enquiry which saw the rapid spread of Islamic civilisation. *'Ilm* (knowledge) was comprehensive and the Holy Prophet (pbuh) came with two distinct roles in human history:

- to terminate the era of prophetic revelation (*wahy*).
- to open the era of modern science which included methodical approach to the study of the Qur'ān and hadith.[45]

Second, it emphasised a fusion of temporal and spiritual endeavours. In other words, the transformation of the human personality at various levels required a spiritual orientation. True *imān*, Mawlānā Ansari stated, belongs to those "who have a personal and direct experience with Allah." Thus, religiosity is a shambolic expression, a 'signboard'[46] that is devoid of the genuine commodities of Islamic values.

In the final anlysis, a pietest approach, in Mawlānā Ansari's estimation, only accessorises Islamic norms and values. This is evident of Muslim insularity in the West. There is a tendency to reject everything linked to Western civilisation ignoring the cultural patterns that are governed by the laws of the historical process. Essentially, culture cannot be separated in the evolution of a community and therefore Muslims are no exception to this rule. Mawlānā Ansari believed that Islam can adjust itself anywhere in a capitalist or communist country.[47] The ideals of the Qur'ān and sunnah have the innate potential to guide Muslims in every situation and under different circumstances of their lives.

Before we attempt to give the broad outlines of Mawlānā Ansari's lecture on *Islam and Communism* delivered at the Stellenbosch

---

[45] Mohamed, *Islam to the Modern Mind*, 28-30.

[46] Ibi., 162.

[47] Mawlānā Ansari' critique of Western civilisation and Communism are a testament to his mastery over these 'isms'.

University, the general Muslim response to the ideological system must be first examined.

A crisis of confidence pervaded academic institutions where the rhetoric of radical change was advocated. Against this backdrop, Islam's response to Communism was marginalised by Muslim intellectuals and students and considered inconsequential. In the absence of `ulamā providinga critique on Communism there was a bleak prospect of challenging its rising presence among Muslims.[48] No doubt, monographs from outside the country were published[49] to repudiate the isms which included Communism but there was a glaring absence of scholarly works. Mawlānā Ansari's academic profile enabled him to make a detailed study of Communism which was intertwined with political developments in Muslim countries. In his view, Communist theories were utopian in practice. It militated against Islam's concept of a social order which "rests on the belief in God, and in an ethical basis of life."[50] Social justice in Islam on the other hand rejected oppressive regimes, emphasised selfless interest which was given a practical demonstration by the Holy Prophet (pbuh) and the *salaf-al-sālih*.Muslims were given explicit advice: follow the Qur'ānic dictum of social justice which entails accountability to Allah and a moral responsibility towards mankind.

Tasawwuf in the Cape: Assessment

An important dimension of Mawlānā Ansari's visit to Cape was his elucidation of *tasawwuf* perspectives in his lectures at mosques and at private *majālis*.[51] The following assessment by Yusuf da Costa of the *tasawwuf* tradition in the Cape is illustrative:

There can be very little doubt that the practice of

---

[48] Interview with Mahdie Kriel (Cape Town), 21/04/2012.

[49] The *Ramadan Annual*, for example, contained articles on *Islam and Communism* by writers from South Asia.

[50] Mohamed, *Islam to the Modern Mind*, 206.

[51] Lecture entitled What is Islam was delivered at Chiappini Street Mosque.

Islam at the Cape, by virtue of its very particular historical circumstances, has been considerably coloured by the *tasawwuf* tradition; and, in a sense, this tradition has added a warmth and fervor to the practice of Islam that is not necessarily found where such a traditionis not flourishing. This has resulted in certain unique community practices and structures being established that are generally associated, in one way or another, with this tradition."[52]

The unique community practices were derived from the *mashā'ikh* of the Arab world who settled in the Cape and retained their distinctive forms of *tasawwuf.* Similarly young Muslims from the Cape who had been sent to different parts of the Islamic world to study *hifdh* or Islamic sciences (*`ulūm*) returned home and did make efforts to encourage the spread of these practices which included *Mawlud al-Nabi,* `urs of awliyā, etc.[53]

Our focus is on the Qādiriyyah order and its relation to *tasawwuf.* The Qādiriyyah had been widespread in the African continent. As the order spread out in different regions, many sub-branches and offshoots also appeared but those were designated by the local Qādiri saints. Although they became better known after the names of their immediate founders, they retained their affiliation to the central figure of the *silsilah,* Shaykh Abdul Qādir Jilāni.[54]

During the latter half of the twentieth century many internationally renowned shaykhs visited South Africa among whom was Mawlānā Siddiqui Al-Qādri who came in 1934 and1952 respectively. There were local sufi shaykhs whose impact also contributed to the growth and development of *tasawwuf* traditions in the Cape. They were affiliated to the Qādiriyyah and other *silsilas*(orders) as well. The multiplicity of orders stemmed from the unitary experience conveyed by the *mashā'ikh* in their quest for promoting the shared ideals of *tasawwuf.*

---

[52] Generally, the *majlis* was held at the home of Haji Zubair Sayed.
[53] Generally, the *majlis* was held at the home of Haji Zubair Sayed.
[54] Da Costa, *Pages from Cape Muslim History,* 139.

The function of the spiritual genealogy (*shajarah*) is succinctly explained by Mawlānā Ansari in the following words:

"We enter the Qādiriyyah Order, or any other order for the sake of spiritual knowledge and practice to become godly. By godly, we mean acquiring as much holiness as possible: to refine our thought, body, soul our entire being. Consequently, we read the *shajarah* to remain in touch with this chain or channel which has been formed by Allah (SWT) for us. When we read the *shajarah* we establish our connection with the Holy Prophet (pbuh) through that chain."[55]

Mawlānā Ansari was the leading exponent of the Qādiriyyah and his lectures in 1970 and 1972 reaffirmed the primacy of *tasawwuf* in Muslim life.

Mawlānā Ansari's definition of *tasawwuf* has been rightly called the spiritual pursuit in Islam. A sufi is one who 'does not He maintained that generally Muslims behave in only the external or formal manifestation of Islam.'[56] In the same vein, he appeals to the believer to blend the spirit of Islam with his actions based on the principle of genuine *imān* (faith) and *ihtisāb* (self-reflection). If this approach is adopted, the human personality will develop harmoniously. As a corollary, the importance of knowledge in respect of oneself, environment and the entire cosmos reaffirms that this world and everything in it is meaningful and purposeful. Therefore, this outlook as exemplified by the Holy Prophet (pbuh), practised and propagated by all his true followers, is the cornerstone of Allah-realisation (*taqwā*). Mawlānā Ansari stated clearly that Islam was not merely something scholarly but could be experienced and internalised and made part and parcel of one's personality.[57] It is the ideal of *ihsān* that *tasawwuf* strives towards; it is the ability to rise and to cultivate one's consciousness in terms of servitude to Allah to a level that the following hadith becomes a reality in one's life:

---

[55] Mohamed, *Islam to the Modern Mind*, 267.
[56] Mohamed, *Islam to the Modern Mind*, 262.
[57] Ibid, 251.

"Serve your Lord as if you are seeing Him and if that is not possible than serve your Lord with the consciousness that Allah is seeing and you are worshipping Him."[58]

According to Mawlānā Ansari, there are three moral virtues, a hierarchy of values per se, that need to be cultivated to experience the inner dimension of Islam. They are truthfulness, honesty and service to mankind. They serve as a guiding spirit to bring spiritual refinement and fervour in one's *ibādah* and interaction with people. The spiritual refinement also cuts the roots of dogmatic and ritualistic demonstration of Islam and enables *tazkiyah* (spiritual growth) in one's journey towards spiritual purification.

Mawlānā Ansari cautions Muslims that *tasawwuf* devoid of the sunnah is of no value. Sunnah refers to a way of life practised by the Holy Prophet (pbuh). Thus inner and outer aspects of life must harmonise to give orientation in all human endeavours. He is criticalof those who marginalise the inner values which become an imageof the Holy Prophet's (pbuh) personality."[59] *Tasawwuf* emphasises the sunnah of inward perfection. In contrast, Muslim obsession for outward appearance deforms and deshapes the intent and spirit of the sunnah.

As a Qādiri shaykh, *Mawlud-al-Nabi* was integral to his elucidation of the *tasawwuf* tradition. According to Yusufda Costa, *Mawlud al-Nabi* was an established practice in the Cape and was given further impetus by several *mashā'ikh* of Arab origin.[60] It was embedded within a *tasawwuf* tradition in which the sublime status of the Holy Prophet (pbuh) was eulogised. MawlānāAnsari's devotion to the personality and the celebration of the Holy Prophet 's (pbuh) birthday (*mawlūd*) are linked to his *islāhi* vision:

...He who is to be revived spiritually and given a new life through

---

[58] Ibid., 248.

[59] Mohamed, *Islam to the Modern Mind*, 101.

[60] Da Costa, *Pages from Cape Muslim History*, 185.

Islam, he should build up that life on the basis of reason (and positive rational pursuit) of the imān... (8: 42)

The Muslim Assembly (Cape Town)

Established in 1967 in the City Hall, Cape Town, the Muslim Assembly was inaugurated in the presence of a distinguished guest, Dr. Ishtiaq Hussain Qureshi, Vice Chancellor of the University of Karachi. Dr. Hoosein Kotwal (d. 2003), a noted Islamic scholar and educationist, undertook the formidable challenge with his dedicated team to address the socio-economic issue affecting the Muslim community in the Cape. Under his dynamic leadership, the Muslim Assembly set about the task of the reformation and reconstruction of the Muslim society at the Cape.

Both Mawlānā Ansari and Dr. Kotwal were alumni of Aligarh Muslim University (AMU) and a strong bond of mutual respect was established between them. Dr. Kotwal's insightful assessment of educational reforms in Muslim institutions was published in *The Minaret* and there was no doubt that Mawlānā Ansari's influence was much in evidence. Mawlānā Suleiman Peterson (Faridi), a graduate of the Aleemiyah Institute made the following observation of Mawlānā Ansari's relationship with the Muslim Assembly:

Dr Ansari was the guest of the Muslim Assembly (Cape) and I remember the occasion on his very first lecture in Cape Town when the organiser, Mr M.T. Ajam and the secretary, Mr S.A. Seria, on requesting the men in the audience to make place for the ladies there was no response. But before Dr. Ansari started his lecture, he said very simply that it was Islam which introduced the concept of 'ladies first' in the world and, as if on a given signal, all the men in the audience stood up to offer their seats to the ladies. This request was greeted with a thundering applause. I vividly remember the opening address of this great orator and the ease with which he recited the Holy Qur'ān which captivated and fascinated me. In the middle of his lecture, I had made up my mind to come to Pakistan and to learn under this man. His lecture was interspersed with clapping from the audience. But the ovation he gotat the end of the lecture was deafening. The people had taken him to their hearts; they loved him. There were a quite a number of non-Muslims in the audience andI learnt afterwards that four people (it might be more) had embraced Islam under him.[61]

The Muslim Assembly's recognition of Mawlānā Ansari's multi-dimensional contributions to the Muslim ummah was expressed in the life patronage conferred on him.

---

[61] *The Minaret*, May 1975, 61.

LIFE PATRONAGE CONFERRED
By
The Muslim Assembly
(Cape, South Africa)

Mawlānā Shah Hafiz Muhammad Fazlur Rahman Ansari Al-Qaderi

Your affectionate concern for the ummah in all parts of the world has enabled us, this Muslim community of the Western Cape Region of the Republic of South Africa, to have the privilege and the singular honour of being visited by you. We thank Almighty Allah for the blessing of having in our midst, regrettably for a short duration, so illustrious a servant of the Ummah of Rasool-e-Kareem Muhammad (PBUH) to teach and inspire us to more resolute action, higher ideals and more dedicated commitment individually and collectively to the Cause of Islam.

Esteemed teacher, guide and mentor of the universal fraternity of Muslims! Your example to us in these troubled times evokes our deep appreciation, our warm affection and highest regard. Our youth, and all who seek understanding of Islam, have cause to rejoice that so eminently qualified a scholar, such an undaunted Mujahid, has, by the Grace of Almighty Allah, restated Islamic values and ethical ideals in meaningful terms, and invigorated our spirits towards the determined pursuit of those ideals.

In a period of uncertainties and wastefulness of human resources, Your Eminence has contributed to Islamic education as an academic discipline in a manner that will restore to the ummah of Rasool-e-Kareem that practice of the pure Islam as its *raison d'etre*, removing from its life the tendency to separate the apparentlyreligious and secular into two compatible entities.

As a humble token of our affection and esteem, and as a commemoration of your historic visit to these shores, we have the honour to bestow upon you the distinction of

LIFE PATRON
OF
THE MUSLIM ASSEMBLY (CAPE)

And we do fervently pray that Almighty Allah will grant you his blessings in abundance upon all your endeavours.

Sept. 1970

Cape Town[62]

****

The Muslim Assembly headed by Dr. Kotwal gave due recognition to Mawlānā Ansari's versatility and also prepared a series of lectures inspired by his multi-faceted personality. Ansari's scholarly exposition was reflective of his Qur'ānic approach in which he drew the audience's attention to the Qur'ān's timeless message to humanity.[63]

---

[62] *The Minaret*, May 1975, 29.
[63] Interview with Hafiz Advocate Abu Bakr Mahomed (Houghton, 10/03/2012).

Second Lecture Visit (1972)

Mawlānā Ansari's second historic visit to South Africa must be examined in the context of Islamic developments in the country. The activities of the Muslim Youth Movement had a direct bearing on Mawlānā Ansari's lectures.

Muslim Youth Movement Background

The founding members of the Muslim Youth Movement (MYM) were inspired to act decisively on several observations about the Islamic experience in South Africa. After three hundred and fifty years of Muslim presence in the country there was no meaningful impact on the indigenous communities to embrace the universal message of Islam. Moreover, ethnicity dominated the worldview of Cape and Indian Muslims who retained their cultural practices derived from the lens of sectarian perception and ethos.

Da'wah had been established on the soil although on a limited scale with different objective. Ahmad Deedat and the Islamic Propagation Centre focused on the Christian missionary threat while the Tabligh Jamā'at had their reformist ideas exclusively for the Muslim community. For younger Muslims in the late 1960s the 'Islam of the Mimbar' was problematic; there was no intelligent understanding of the Qur'ān that had contemporary relevance for them. A parallel development during this period was the unprecedented embracing of the Marxist ideology which then was perceived as synonymous with the liberation struggle.

Two concerns emerged during the crucial period: the absence of structured Islamic programmes for the upliftment of the *ummah* and Muslim communities living in self-enclosed pockets.

It was against this backdrop of events the founding members undertook the daunting task to launch the MYM. As a resurgent Islamic movement, its broad mandate was to consolidate a vibrant collective Islamic identity and articulate it in modern and rational discourse.

The MYM was formed by three individuals in Durban 1970. Ebrahim Jadwat, a young businessman from Durban who had been actively associated with the Arabic Study Circle was supported by Mahmud Moosa, also a young businessman from Durban to establish the structure of the organisation.

Hafiz Abu Bakr Mahomed, a law graduate of the Universityof Durban-Westville, was the third and most charismatic founder. During the formative period of the organisation, he was the most 'eloquent and articulate spokesperson.' Other influential members of Gauteng included Ismail Kalla of Pretoria and Shawkat Thokan of Rustenburg.

Early Vision of the MYM

The MYM envisaged a programme of action that sought to elucidate and enlighten the ummah, particularly the youth, about a progressive Islam that did not reflect the legal minutiae advocated by ʿulamā. They were motivated by an Islamic ideology to chart a new course for the ummah. Outside the periphery of a traditional understanding of Islam, Islamist movements led by Sayyid Qutb (d. 1966) of Egypt and Sayyid Abul Aʿlā Mawdudi (d. 1979) of Pakistan provided alternative readings of Islam as *dīn*. Their respective writings captured "the basic elements of the Islamic paradigm of the twentieth century" and enjoyed the widest appeal among modern educated youth. The MYM was not immune to the ideological currents of Islamic resurgence advocated by these two scholars.

MYM Convention: As-Salam

The first Convention was held at As-Salam, the training centre operated by Ahmad Deedat and the Islamic Propagation Centre. Mawlānā Ansari was invited to deliver a series of inspirational lectures. The recurrent themes on the status of the Holy Prophet (pbuh), spiritual evolution and unity in Islam were extremely popular. One of Mawlānā Ansari's lectures *Unity in Islam* (Ittihād-fil-Islam) was recorded and distributed throughout the country. Ismail Kalla was largely responsible for the production of the lecture into a long-playing record.

Mawlānā Ansari represented 'a crystallisation of the modern and traditional in contemporary Islam' owing to his proficiency in philosophy, Qur'ānic tafsir and l Islamic law. For the MYM he was the exemplary person who mirrored in his knowledge and approach the aspirations of the organisation.

The successive Conventions brought scholars from overseas who were non-`ulamā. They too stressed the unity of Islam and its relevance to the modern world and the need for active involvement and commitment to the Islamic cause. Mawlānā Ansari's lecture *Message to the Muslim Youth* was preceded by a message from the MYM's president, Hafiz Abu Bakr Mahomed. His eloquence and candid assessment of the realities facing the Muslim community in South Africa received laudable comments from Mawlānā Ansari. Three pertinent points emerged from his excellent message:

- Muslims lived in a world of insularity which thwarted efforts for meaningful interaction and disseminating the message of Islam to non-Muslims

- The promotion of Islamic ideals anchored on intellectual and spiritual dynamism was impeded by Muslim attachment to 'traditional values' perceived as Islamic.

- Institutions established by the earlier generations in the country needed to be overhauled to foster the ideal Islamicsociety.

Mawlānā Ansari's elaboration of Hafiz Abu Bakr's critique of the Muslim community revolved around three issues. First, the value system Islam brought was based on the principle of unity (*tawhīd*). But it was 'inner wrangling' linked to a history of `*ilm-al kalām* (dialectical philosophy) that created schools of thought whichin turn created sub-divisions on account of promoting a schismatic ideology at the expense of Muslim unity. Second, Muslims needed to *rediscover* the whole of Islam which represents the harmonious blending of all values and dimensions of life. Last, the Muslim youth as ambassadors of Islam needed to re-align their lives on the value system of Islam as given in the Qur'ān and sunnah. "In the Holy Qur'ān and the life of the Holy Prophet (pbuh) is a philosophy of life which is magnanimous, broadminded, enlightened, progressive, dynamic and revolutionary." This approach removed pre-conceived opinions and inherited misunderstanding about Islam .

Hafiz Abu Bakr's assessment of Mawlānā Ansari's lectures represented the three stages in a Muslim's journey towards Divine Pleasure. It is articulated in the textual tradition through the Qur'ānwhich is the infallible guide for mankind (`ilm al-bayān). The foundation of Islamic spiritual tradition (`ilm-al-irfān) is based on *tazkiyah* (spiritual purification) which is an integral component of a believer's journey to Divine realisation. The rational sciences (`ilm al-burhān) serve as a conduit for a sustainable Islamic civilisation.

According to Hafiz Abu Bakr the shari`ah negated the schizophrenic display of Islam where outward expression was alienated from inner perfection. Mawlānā Ansari was the living embodiment of the Qur'ānic view of the perfect man (*insān-al-kāmil*). *Living Islam* is thus closely associated with the quality of *ihsān*. It is the re-awakening of the human personality that is influenced by shari`ah and *tariqah*. Shari`ah is the outward manifestation that can function within a *tariqah* framework. Conversely tariqah devoid of substantive meaning and vision can lead to myriad forms of irreligosity. Mawlānā Ansari's philosophy contained in his lectures reinforced this approach. It is this spirit that transformational knowledge can adequately prepare transformational leadership.

Likewise, Ismail Kalla's deep-seated admiration for Mawlānā Ansari stemmed from the latter's exposition of transformation. Mawlānā Ansari categorically stated that levels of transformation if applied within the framework of the Qur'ān and sunnah will not only ensure potential growth for the ummah in all facets of life but will also signpost humanity's destiny in the future. Ismail Kalla expresses a similar thought.

> "Transformation is initiated with a passionate intention to change, before we can take on the challenges of life. If one commences the journey to change, Almighty Allah and His angels support and sustain the believer with Blessings, Mercy and Guidance."[64]

Mawlānā Ansari encouraged Islamic organisations like the MYM to establish movements which would exemplify Islam as a *dīn*, an all-encompassing way of life. The Islamic Da`wah Movement, South Africa National Zakah Fund (SANZAF), were representative of MYM's commitment to create an ideal Islamic ideology.

Unity in Islam: Message

It would be worthwhile to locate Mawlānā Ansari's final lecture *Unity in Islam* within the broader framework of theological differences found in both South Africa and the Indian subcontinent. The Qur'ānic verses (*āyāt*) to which Mawlānā Ansari referred in his lecture emphasised the principle of unity as a code of life. The following āyah has a clear-cut implication:

> *Hold fast to the bond of unity which Allah has created in the ummah and never divide yourselves into sects or groups on any grounds whatsoever.*

> (3:103)

In connection with religious groups which have been formed on the basis of intolerance and the projection of individual egos, Mawlānā Ansari's message is unambiguous:

---

[64] Kalla, *Unleash Your Potential*, 4.

"The only solution for this small community in South Africa is to drown all differences for the sake of Allah and love for the Holy Prophet (pbuh) who is our only leader and to whom we owe a pledge of loyalty."[65]

Mawlānā Ansari's position on the inter-school disputation was clear, he rejected a sectarian approach to doctrinal issues. In this regard he said:

"I am neither Wahhābi, nor Deobandi, neither Ahl al- Hadith nor Barelvi. I am only Muslim."

As a roving ambassador of Islam, he expressed these courageous words in the 1970s, and its relevance can still 'build the bridge over which this ummah can cross the chasm of theological conflict and disunity.' The following excerpts of Mawlānā Ansari's public lectures indicate his pragmatic approach to the *ikhtilāf* (difference of opinion) problem. Instead of condemning the religious groups, Mawlānā Ansari pointed out alternatives in preserving the unity of the *ummah:*

Here the Holy Qur'ān does not mention all those over-indulgences which later Muslims developed in orderto fight one another and to come to blows and to call one another *kāfir* (disbeliever). I do not wish to excite trouble but I know, unfortunately, that there are some among the ʿulamā who talk for the sake of mischief only. I am not a professional ʿālim or preacher and I don't belong to any group. I belong to only group and that is Islam – the group of the Holy Prophet (pbuh). The Sunni Muslims of India and Pakistan have been divided into two perpetual hostile camps about this issue. The problem is really very simple one and I don't know why it has not been resolved. And different groups are arising with their

---

[65] Mohamed, Islam to the Modern Mind, 180.

own interpretation of Muhammad (pbuh), I don't blame them. I do not standin hall condemning this group as a *mushrik* and that group as a *kāfir* and this group is this and that group is that. I don't believe in all this because I realise as a very humble student, as a very humble pursuer of knowledge that knowledge has different levels. Everybody's level of knowledge is not that same that he may be calledan *aalim-e-deen* (knowledgeable in religion) or he may be called anything else. The comprehension of knowledge varies from one person to another. These confusions arise only because those who come forward to understand the problem, try to view it with all their subjective limitations.

According to Mawlānā Ansari Muslims have failed to grasp the true content of *tawhid* in faith and practice. He says:

But Islam is a theme of unity and we should try to understand it on the basis of the life of the Holy Prophet (pbuh) in how to transform human beings.It is, what was and what should be the processto be adopted, in order that we may undertake the process for ourselves, as individuals and our communities. Stick to this *Al Kitāb wa Sunnah* (Qur'ān and sunnah) and thus we will have a smooth sailing. To abstain from division - that is the command in the Holy Qur'ān. We should firstly concern ourselves with things that are of primary importance.

When I say that we should curb this ritualism, disunity and fighting about small issues, we should rather try to imbibe the Islamic spirit. This does notmean that any of the foundations can be given up at any time or in any manner. Whatever has been prescribed and accepted by the Ahle Sunnah wa'l Jamā`ah, which has always been the overwhelming majority of Muslims, this is the real and genuine Islam and correct. The only mistake that we have made is in connection with its practice in that we have sometimes put the cart before the horse."[66]

Conclusion

Mawlānā Ansari's return to Pakistan after his second visit to South Africa (1972) was marked by an elaborate Welcome Reception.The message read:

"We are gathered here today to welcome back our great warrior from his conquest of South Africa – a conquest achieved on the battlefield of ideas in one and single combat and without a soldier at his side to fight with him."

The *battlefield of ideas* contained in Mawlānā Ansari's inspirational lectures "were boulders thrown into the stagnant poolof the minds of the South African Muslim community, the sound of which reverberates to this day."

---

[66] Kriel, *Islamic Intellectual Revival of the Modern World* (Cape Town, 2011), 208.

Mawlānā Ansari's Lecture Programmes in South Africa: 1970

Durban/Pietermaritzburg

22 August: Juma Mosque (Grey Street).
23 August: Orient Hall (Welcome Reception).
24 August: Meeting with Professionals and Leading Business Figures.
Lecture at the West Street Mosque.
25 August: Mohammediya Mazjid, Sparks Road, Overport
Lecture: *Meaning and Significance of Salāh.*
26 August: Juma Mosque (hosted by Buzme Ikwanus Suffa).
Lecture: *Education - An Islamic Perspective.*
27 August: Juma Mosque.
Lecture: *Lofty Status of the Holy Prophet (pbuh).*
24-27 August: Nizami Building of A.M.Khan.
 Topic: *Question and Answer Sessions.*
28 August: Orient Hall.
Topic: *General for Ladies.*
29 August: Iqbalia Mosque (Chatsworth).
Topic: *Love for the Holy Prophet (pbuh).*
30 August: A.I.Timol Residence (La Mercy)
Guest Speaker: *Mawlud al-Nabi* function.
31 August: Visit to Howard College (University of Natal). Topic: *Informal Discussions with Faculty.*
Flower Road Mosque (Clairwood).
Topic: *Muslim Commitment to the Teachings of Islam.*
1 September: Visit to the M.L. Sultan College.
Lecture at the Jainah Hall (Stanger).
2 September: Westville University (renamed University of KwaZulu-Natal).
Topic: *Why Religion.*
3 September: Civic Hall (Ispingo).
Topic: *Islam and Human Dignity.*
4 September: Verulam Mosque.
Topic: *Islam the Religion of Goodwill.*

5 September: Q@A Session with Medical Fraternity.
Topic: *Islamic Perspective on Pertinent Medical Issues.*
6 September: Avalon Cinema (Durban).
Topic: *Iqbal and the Holy Prophet (pbuh).*
7 September: Juma Mosque.
Topic: *Dimensions of Tasawwuf.*
8 September: Muslim Women's Cultural Group (Durban).
 Topic: Q@A Session.
Lotus Hall (Pietermaritzburg).
Topic: *Islam the Universal Religion.*
9 September: Howard College (University of Natal).
Topic: *Islam and Marxism.*
12 September: Durban City Hall.
Topic: *Islam's Contributions to Human Civilisation.*

Gauteng

13 September: Welcome by Pretoria Muslim Brigade.
Welcome Reception: Pretoria Islamic Society.
14 September: Laudium Mosque.
Topic: *Unity of God.*
15 September: Newtown Musjid,
(Central Islamic Trust, Johannesburg).
Topic: *Unity in Islam.*
16 September: Civic Centre (Laudium).
Topic: *Islam and Marxism.*
17 September: Church Street Mosque (Pretoria).
Topic: *General Issues Relating to Muslim Community of South Africa.*
19 September: Welcome Reception by Aligarh Old Boys' Association
of South Africa. (Nana Memorial Hall, Johannesburg).
Topic: *Q@A Session.*
20 September: Y.M.M.A. (Davies Centre, Benoni).
Topic: *Why Religion.*

Cape Town

21 September: Welcome Reception (*Cape Town City Hall*).

22 September: Drill Hall.
Topic: *Belief and Practice in Islam.*
23 September: Muir Street Mosque (Muslim Judicial Council).
Topic: *Unity in Islam.*
24 September: Stellenbosch University.
Topic: Islam and Communism.
Dhikr programme at Grassy Park Mosque.
25 September: Azzawiya Mosque (Majlis Ashura al-Islami).
Topic: *The Challenge of the 20th Century.*
26 September: Symposium at University of Cape Town Jameson Hall.
Topic: *Do the Different Religions in the World offer a Solution to the Problems of the 20th Century?*
27 September: Stone Laying Ceremony at Bonteheuwel Mosque.
Urs lecture at Habibia Mosque.
Lecture: *What is Tasawwuf* at Chiappini Street Mosque.
28 September: Park Town Road Mosque.
Topic: *Mi'rāj.*
29 September: Habibia Muslim School.
Topic: *Discussion on educational matters.*
30 September: Visit to Muslim Assembly office.
1 October: Elsies River Civic Centre.
Topic: *Crisis of Muslim Identity.*
2 October: Siddique Mosque.
Topic: *Juma'ah Khutbah.*

Lecture Series in South Africa: 1970 and 1972

The Challenge of the Twentieth Century

There are two conflicting impulses that have shaped the Muslim response to the challenges of the twentieth century: philosophy of life and politics. Both of these have taken on ideological forms and impacted significantly the course of events of this century.

The philosophy of life has different meanings for different faith groups. Only certain aspects are incorporated in their respective worldviews. In contrast, this term has a comprehensive meaning and covers all aspects of human activity in Islam which is termed *din*. In a historical sense, the revolutionary message of Islam changed the political and religious landscapes of countries under their sway. Thus, several regions in Africa became Arabised and Islamised, strengthening the spread of Islam through political conquests. People accepted Islam in huge numbers by witnessing the intrinsic good and beauty the Muslims portrayed in their lives. The case of Spain (Andalusia) offers an interesting example about the impact of Islamic culture and civilisation under Muslim rule. It inaugurated a scientific era in a dark period characterised by the conflict of faith and reason in Christianity in which the Church was directly involved. For Muslims, the twin concept of faith and reason was embedded in the knowledge paradigm (*iqrā*) as envisaged by Islam.

Over the centuries the rigid mindset of the Church created a religious void and the drift towards materialism was inevitable. What followed next was a godless society being alienated from the all-embracing virtues promoted by Islam. The rise of political powers with distinctive ideologies - materialism and communism - brought into sharp focus the cleavage between faith and irreligiousness. Muslims were urged to combat the forces of darkness and be a powerful front to assert the supremacy of Islam. In this context, power is considered a virtue whereas weakness is deemed a vice.

Sadly, modern civilisation has sapped the vitality of the Muslim youth so much that moral and spiritual inertia has become the norm. There is no longer the intellectual legacy of giants like Al-Ghazāli (d. 1111) or a spiritual luminary in the calibre of Shaykh Abdul Qādir

Jilāni (d. 1166) who brought about an impactful revolution in the Muslim societies of the day. What is required is the spark of *imān* (faith) that can rekindle our bond with the personality of the Holy Prophet (pbuh). *Imān* can leverage our intellectual temperament and restore our confidence in presenting the eternal message of Islam to humanity.

The growing despondency among Muslims – a negative trait – can only be overcome if they restore their link with the Qur'ānic message: *"... do not despair of Allah's mercy."* (39: 53). Again, they have to turn to Allah with faith and conviction (*yaqin*) in the full knowledge that *imān* is the deciding factor of their future. Islam promotes positive living and interacting with others, especially non-Muslims, in a spirit of tolerance, love and goodwill. Our present-day realities should not be a barrier to acknowledge what is good from others which can be assimilated for the benefit of humanity. Likewise, evil characteristics should be exposed; otherwise, they will lead to the path of Ignorance (*sabil al-jāhiliyyah*).

Pessimism erodes positivity and weakens a believer's trust and faith in Allah. In these bleak moments the Holy Qur'ān offers a refreshing message:

Turn to your Lord, approach Him, come near Him and bow to His will.
(39: 54)

Every Muslim should study Islam and the Qur'ān. Study the message. Let us investigate for ourselves and we will find that Islam is the only panacea (universal cure) for the ills and problems of mankind. Islam is that alchemy that can turn base metals into gold. Islam can benefit us in this life and the Hereafter. The seeker will then acquire real *imān*. Islam did not come to wage war but to advise positive thinking, to invite others with love and affection, with sympathy and the best of goodwill.

Allah is the Truth (*al-haqq*) and therefore our actions should reflect truthfulness (*sidq*) in all circumstances. In this respect the threat to our value system can be countered with the weapons of virtue, Allah-consciousness (*taqwā*) and sacrifice. The state of greatness can only be achieved through humility and godliness as opposed to arrogance and vice.

The Muslim community should not think that the unfavourable conditions pitted against them are signs of terminal decline. On the contrary, these conditions are indicative of the throes of a rebirth. Pain is temporary while the future holds out promises of optimism and renewal of the Islamic culture and civilisation. This is clearly brought out in the Qur'ānic *āyah* (verse):

> *"The forces of evil want to extinguish with their mouths the light that Allah has sent, but He is going to perfect this light even though the unbelievers detest it."*

> (61: 8)

The invitation from Allah is there and it depends on us to take up the challenge.

Knowledge and the Self

The mission of Islam is based on conquest at three levels:

- conquest of the self
- conquest of the environment
- conquest of nature

It is important to remember that Islam as a way of life (*din*) is comprehensive; therefore, there is no distinction between worldly and other-worldly pursuits.

Tazkiyah (self-purification) is an important marker in the development of one's personality and it is the first level on the conquest of the self. It fully recognises the highs and lows or the conflicting impulses that reside in man. Several verses (*āyāt*) of the Qur'ān highlight the necessity of overcoming the baser self (*nafs al-ammārah*) in order to develop a holistic personality. This is no easy path to rightfully become *Khalifat Allah* (custodian of Allah) as it requires rigorous discipline to conquer the baser self. On a broader level, the instinctive self is dominant in man and desires wealth, power and pleasure. When it appears in the form of a raging storm, then man becomes a brute. Constant struggle and perseverance against these desires is termed as *jihād al-akbar* (the greatest striving).

The human personality has two facets: light and darkness, good and evil. The following *āyah* explains it fully:

> *He who permits his personality to become stunted or falls prey to evil,*
> *is a hopeless failure.*

(91:10)

Therefore, the purpose of human life is to realise the potential of *Khalifat Allah*. In other words, man has to follow the straight path as outlined in the Qur'ān and the noble example of the Holy Prophet (pbuh) and not deviate from it. This, in essence, is conquest of the self.

The second level is conquest of the environment. The individual lives in a social order and has to interact with others in a conducive environment. Thus, the purity of the environment which is free from toxic elements makes it possible for the individual to eradicate all types of moral and spiritual evils. The following *āyah* states clearly the function of the *ummah:*

> *You are the best community that has been raised for mankind. You enjoin what is right and forbid (eradicate) evil and you believe in Allah.*

(3: 110)

The individual and collective efforts to cultivate Allah-awareness (*taqwā*) require an equilibrium or a synergy of values that makes it possible to create the ideal Islamic environment. The Qur'ān states clearly:

> *You are the best community that has been raised for mankind. You enjoin what is right and forbid (eradicate) evil and you believe in Allah.*

(3: 110)

The third level of conquest relates to nature. The cosmos points out to the vastness of space which requires knowledge and expertise to probe into the grand design of Allah's creation. Again, the Qur'ān reminds mankind to explore the universe in order to understand the deep meaning of *Khalifat Allah.* In the words of the Qurān:

> *Allah has (endowed the human beings with such power and) made the constitution of everything in the heavens and the earth in such a fashion, so as to be controlled and conquered by man (Allah has made this as the mission of mankind). In these are guidelines for those who ponder and use their intellectual powers.*

(45: 13)

In this connection the Holy Qur'ān speaks of a system of values which is innate to the human personality. These are:

- spiritual (consciousness of a transcendental being)
- aesthetical (beauty and ugliness)
- intellectual (knowledge)
- moral
- physical

It is only in Islam that these values have a harmonious balance in comparison to other communities or cultures that lack this hierarchy of values.

In Islam the quest of knowledge, secular and religious, is emphasised. In the heyday of Islamic civilisation, distinguished Islamic scholars who made a mark in Islamic sciences had mastery over the various branches of secular knowledge. In fact, the madrasah was the site of holistic learning. Over the centuries this prestigious institution fell into decline; now this institution offers only Islamic education. This dismal state of affairs was glaringly visible during the expulsion of the Muslims from Spain (Andalusia) and the fall of Baghdad.

Islamic strongly advocates the fusion of faith and reason and the Qur'ān constantly reminds us of the importance of `ilm (knowledge). Sadly, the Muslim community is caught up in rituals where calculator reward has overwhelmed their mindset. As a result, intellectual stagnation has set in and offers no prospects of Islamic renewal. Education is no longer the prized possession of Muslims and they therefore suffer an inferiority complex. In fact, it will become a memory of the past and Muslims will remain debased.

There Muslims who raise slogans for an Islamic state. However, they tend to forget that in the caliphate of the righteous khulafā the dynamic character of Islam in al facets of life were entrenched. Sectarian differences and ego-bloating interests were rooted out so that the Islamic state could flourish in the ideals of Islam.

For the ummah the message is clear:

O Muslims, take care before Islam becomes a memory of the past. Unless and until we can organise education according to the Islamic concept, and produce God-fearing, morally integrated, spiritually elevated, intellectually enlightened Muslims in this community, we will have no future.

The Principle of Unity (*Tawhīd*)

The principle of unity (*tawhīd*) is a recurring theme in understanding the comprehensive dimensions of Islam. *Tawhid* is a rallying point to unite mankind on a single platform and thus all values flow from it.

Those who accept the divine trust from Allah are expected to follow the mission as laid down in the Qur'ān:

> *You are the best ideological group raised by Allah for the service of mankind (in order that you may be a witness to the divine truth for mankind. That you invite and guide mankind to the path of truth). You command only that which is good and eradicate with all the forces at your command, all that is evil and believe in Allah.*
>
> (3: 110)

Unfortunately, the division amongst Muslims on sectarian basis means that they have deviated from the true meaning of *tawhīd*; thus, the consequences of conflict and petty egos are glaringly evident. Muslim community embodies the spirit of absolute unity that transcends geography and culture. The Holy Qur'ān warns the Muslim community against this unacceptable behaviour:

> *Do not quarrel on the basis on the basis of your personalities; this division will weaken you and your prestige will vanish.*
>
> (8: 46)

However, when the clash of vested interests takes precedence then it is human nature to project one's ego. It is the *nafs al-ammārah* that is embedded in the human personality which gives rise to conflicts and dissension. This attitude downplays the universal role of the Holy Prophet (pbuh) in our lives who is the exemplary role model (*uswah al-hasanah*).

The Qur'an says that the community of Islam that has been raised with this mission is not based on race, language, territory or colour. It is a community based on an ideal towards which they strive to achieve under one banner. The Companions of the Holy Prophet (pbuh) heard the message, thought about it, assimilated it and absorbed it into their personalities and forgot about their egos.

Therefore, the ideal of Islam is to instil the highest of virtue – the virtue of truth combined with sincerity and integrity. Surah Ikhlās embodies the truth of *tawhīd* which is the Muslim's *'aqidah* in Allah. Essentially, belief in Islam is not belief unless it is clearly and positively proclaimed with one's tongue and considered as truth with sincerity and integrity by the heart.

Another serious problem affecting the unity of the *ummah* is the aimless theological questioning and bickering. It takes on a sectarian slant and what follows is the endless *kufr*-bashing that these groups indulge in.

The history of Islam shows that Islam brought about a revolutionary change in the lives of the warring Arab tribes and welded them into a single brotherhood - a lasting achievement of Islam. Essentially, anyone who becomes a believer has to interact with a fellow brother on the basis of *tawhīd*. The Qur'ān says that the Muslim community has been raised with this mission of solidarity – an *ummatic* responsibility for the betterment of mankind. If, however, individuals want to insulate themselves and work solely for Islam then it has no merit in the eyes of Allah.

In Islam the highest virtue is to promote truth combined with sincerity and integrity. Moral truth is embedded in *tawhīd* and is non-negotiable. Belief in Islam is not belief unless it is clearly and positively proclaimed with one's tongue and considered as truth by the heart. It is hypocrisy to say one thing and do another thing resulting in violating the Commands of Allah. In contrast, the community of Islam was built by the Holy Prophet (pbuh) on the solid foundation of *imān billah*: these were the Sahābah who challenged the mightiest empires of the day that the whole world trembled before them while they were just a handful.

The history of Islam highlights the glorious eras of Islamic civilisation. Centuries of Muslim conquest also witnessed a gradual decline due to a number of historical and other factors. Disunity was more pronounced as in the case of the fall of the Muslim empire in Spain. Governors with vested interests in Spain (Andalusia) wanted to rule the empire even if meant colluding with the enemies of Islam.

Likewise, Muslim rule in the Indian subcontinent (977-1857) suffered a similar fate: traitors like Mir Sadiq conspired against the Mughal empire during British rule of the subcontinent.

The degradation of the ummah has witnessed a tragic turn of events in occupied Palestine. King Hussein of Jordan had enlisted the support of Israel in complicit with United States (US) to protect his autocratic rule. Two enemies of Islam who since 1948 have been responsible for the ethnic cleansing of Palestinians!

Our lives are a series of fleeting shadows – dreams – and nothing beyond that. This is the reality of *hayat al-dunya* as described in several *ayat* of the Qur'an. This life is like the stock of an ice vendor. He buys the ice from the factory and invests capital in order to gain profit. But he gets that much of money according to the capital he invests. The portion that turns into water is lost in the earth and is unclaimable. Likewise, is the fleeting nature of our lives.

We need to understand the tragic consequences of disunity in the light of the Qur'an and sunnah. Our principal enemy is our ego. When it is unchecked, it can cause havoc in the Muslim world. We are deceived in believing that our ego is the dominant force in this world, forgetting that it will be held accountable before Allah. In this strain, Muslim leaders with bloated egos will not be immune from the severe punishment of Allah in the Afterlife because of their domineering behaviour and forcibly misguiding Muslim masses.

The Age of Doubt: An Overview

This century (twentieth century) is in marked contrast with the nineteenth century which was regarded as an age of faith. In a historical process it has undergone fundamental changes and is dubbed as the age of doubt. The universe is conservative in the sense that it has retained its fundamental character while changing according to Allah's divine laws. In a similar way, the Muslim community is exposed to changes - forces of historical compulsion - that require adaptation. In this respect, the youth are caught in the crossfire of ultra-conservatism and ultra-modernism. Conservatism is a virtue but when it is taken beyond its limits it is a vice.

The philosophy of change states clearly that the pursuit of knowledge is tied up with man's advancement in the world. If he flies on the wings of knowledge then he soars to greater heights. Discoveries lead to harnessing the natural resources for the advancement of a better economic life. So is with science and technology, by bringing about qualitative changes. Overall, the caravan of life spurs man to move ahead and embrace change without sacrificing the fundamentals that govern our collective life.

Sadly, in the Muslim community the pietists have resisted real and meaningful changes, declaring them to be *harām*. This mindset, living in a shell, has impacted negatively the Muslim ummah whose population now exceeds 1.8 billion adherents. They have no international status and the result is that that other countries are exploiting our weaknesses for their vested interests.

Muslims have built superstitions and shells around Islam that it is unable to penetrate those false barriers. In this respect, Muslims have built a cult that is dogmatic, ritualistic and is devoid of ethical considerations. In Pakistan, for example, pure honey is imported because only adulterated honey is available in the markets which are controlled by the *hājis*. Parents are too concerned about acquiring wealth and as a result neglect their children's upbringing. Another malaise is the of *zakāh* in the month of *Ramadān*. Wealthy merchants will be seen with this heap of money in front of them for the purpose of distribution. Then a whole army of undignified Muslim beggars in dirty and tattered clothes will swarm the market places of Karachi, receiving paltry amounts from the *zakāh* disbursement. This is a deplorable situation and against the ethical principles of Islam. The Holy Prophet (pbuh) established for the first time in history a welfare state that undertook to guarantee the basic needs of every member of the Muslim community. Social justice was the defining factor and committed the Muslim community to the highest Islamic ideal as mentioned in the following Qur'ānic *āyah* (verse):

"Allah has purchased from the believers their life and their wealth, in lieu of deferred payment, Jannah (Paradise)."

(9: 111)

Allah is the real Owner, Creator and Maintainer of everything. The secondary ownership that we acquire has to be surrendered to Allah in order to be a believer. It entails a sacrifice of one's wealth for the pleasure of Allah. This is in clear contrast to 'trading' in which certain *tasbihs* are read on a particular night to earn exponential reward. This calculator mentality is meant to obtain *jannah* with zero investment. The prestige and glory of Islam is not built on ritualistic practices that are very much evident in the Muslim community. On the contrary, real love is deepened in the unconditional and unwavering love for Allah: *"The believers are those who are strong in their love for Allah* (2: 165).

The Muslim community is the microcosm of a Muslim country; it is vulnerable to the technological manipulation of the superpowers. They control Muslim countries in more ways than one and dictate policies that show their abject subservience to their imperialistic designs. For example, the superpowers want the Zionist state of Israel to remain as a dagger in the heart of the Arab world. It is a tragedy that Muslim countries have lagged behind in the field of science and technology and their presence is considered inconsequential in the comity of nations. By contrast, it was the Holy Prophet (pbuh) who inaugurated the scientific era, the promotion of the inductive method, and Muslims in the past made phenomenal progress in this respect. Several Orientalist writings have acknowledged the Muslims' contributions to science and technology in their heyday. The first message of the Qur'ān gave the impetus to the acquisition of knowledge in a systematic form:

"Read in the name of your Lord who created - created man out of a germ cell. Read - for your Lord is the Most Bountiful One who has taught the use of the pen - taught man what he did not know."

(96: 1-5).

The first message came for *'ilm* (knowledge): the function of this will be to unearth all the treasures of knowledge that are buried in the different civilisations of the world. It entails the following: to preserve, to classify and to rectify all the different types of knowledge and advance the cause of knowledge. Unfortunately, the literacy rate in many Muslim countries is a sad reflection of Muslims' apathy to acquire knowledge in the various fields of learning.

There is a general tendency among Muslims to explain the meaning of the term *din* in a narrow sense. Dogmas and rituals are a pale reflection of Islam as a *din* – the complete way of life. In the South African context, Islam has not been fully grasped by the youth and this explains their disenchantment with the concept of *din*. Instead, they have been exposed to a barrage of *fatwās* that are incompatible to their religious disposition. Against this background, it is important to build up the fortress of Islam among the youth so that they may develop into better human beings and be able to show the torch of guidance to others. At the same time, the Islamic ideals need to be fostered among the youth so that they may be true representatives of the Muslim community.

Among the major concerns facing the Muslim community in the country is upgrading the standards in the madrasahs. These are the bastions of Islam and need to prepare the youth against the hostile forces that create doubts in their minds. Therefore, it is important that the youth are given a balanced education, Islamic and secular, which is reflective of the dynamic and revolutionary message imparted to the ummah by the Holy Prophet (pbuh) and embedded in the Qur'ānic teaching: *"Our Lord, give us the best of this world and the best in the Afterlife..."* (2: 201).

The Muslim community is urged to return to the dynamic, progressive teachings of the Qur'ān which are the real Islam as opposed to 'sophisticated foolishness' practised in the name of Islam. For the South African Muslims, the message is clear: turn back to the source of life (Islam) to become a beacon of light and guidance for other communities. This can only be possible if they bring in their lives the qualities of godliness (*taqwā*), absolute justice, truth, beauty, wisdom and holiness. The Qur'ānic message has resonance for all times in this āyah: *...You will be superior if you are believers.* (3: 139)

We should take stock of the entire situation and teach our youth and create those agencies (platforms) whereby they can acquire the real Islam. And the real Islam is so fascinating, charming and beautiful, that if it is offered to anyone, the person will never refuse it. That is our duty cure for our present malady.

The Inner Dimension of Sunnah

Islam over the years has been reduced to a cult with the result that ritual practices have been given undue importance. In other words, there is more emphasis on the outer aspects rather than the inner aspects and as such the harmony that Islam emphasises is lost in our daily lives. In addition, this mindset diminishes the importance of Isam as a way of life.

Consider the outward forms of the sunnah that Muslim practise by ignoring the spirit that are associated with them. For example, growing a beard should be a signboard of one's love of Islam and ensuring that one's behaviour does not contradict the spirit behind this sunnah. Sadly, the sunnah has been distorted that even a genuine love for the Holy Prophet (pbuh) is not displayed fully. Moreover, the inner dimensions of the sunnah are ignored and also compromised.

Taqwā forms an essential part of Islamic virtues. It is to revere Allah in His Majesty and be mindful of one's accountability to Him. It is meant to develop Allah-awareness at all times and in all circumstances. It cultivates positive behaviour and develops qualities of compassion, empathy, justice etc.

The highest level of *taqwā* is best illustrated in the beautiful example of the Holy Prophet (pbuh). In his *tahajjud* salāh, his devotion to Allah was absolute. According to our Mother of the Faithful, Sayyidah A'isha (may Allah be pleased with her) the feet of the Holy Prophet (pbuh) would swell to the extent that capillaries would burst causing blood to flow. Love for Allah, personified in his long hours of salāh demonstrated the true essence of *taqwā*.

What is the quality of our salāh? It is performed ritualistically with no elements of focus, devotion and presence of heart. It does not activate our love and reverence of Allah; it lacks depth and heart-to-heart conversation with Allah. Likewise, there is no progress in terms of our connection with the *Rabb al-Ālamin* – the Lord of the worlds.

Again, we are reminded that the inner aspects of the sunnah must not be neglected! Otherwise, the outward form of the sunnah is like having a timber wall where the wood is infested with white ants. A case in point is when Muslims rest in the afternoons (sometimes, lengthy hours) and say it is sunnah. Yet the Holy Prophet (pbuh) was the most hardworking and industrious person born in the history of mankind. He used to work the whole day taking care of all the affairs of the ummah, and in order to make `ibādah for the rest of the night, he would generally take a power nap to regain his energy for *tahajjud* salāh. By contrast, our degenerating attitude distorts the original practice of the sunnah. Therefore, love for the Holy Prophet (pbuh) can only be realised if the outward form of the sunnah reflects its inner dimension. The Arabic word used in the hadith literature is *bātin* (inner expression).

Coming back to *taqwā:* if you have the fear the accountability (*ihtisāb*) before Allah then you cannot do any wrong. You cannot lose sight of the fact that Allah is watching us and will call us to account on the Day of Judgement (*Qiyāmah*). Therefore, the starting point of the sunnah is to internalise human values like truth, justice, beauty, honesty, courage in our lives. This is the sunnah of the Holy Prophet (pbuh).

The sunnah is actually the transformation of the heart, on the basis of all those human values which reached their perfection in the Holy Prophet (pbuh). The start is from the inner-self and has to be built up first; then the external manifestation of those great qualities will automatically come.

The inner dimensions of the sunnah are also interlinked with *tasawwuf.* Thus, a sufi is a Muslim whose ideal in life is aligned to the purification of the heart (*safā al-qalb*). The spiritual perfection which was granted to the Holy Prophet (pbuh) by Allah is uniquely associated to him.

The goal of Islam is to build up a vibrant, living, dynamic relationship with Allah which is the focal point in Islam. Once this flame of love is kindled in a person's heart then the external behaviour will reflect this deep relationship with Allah.

In sum, preach love for Allah and the Holy Prophet (pbuh) alone as it is the source of moral and spiritual perfection.

Philosophy of the Shahādah

The universal message of revealed more than fourteen hundred years ago was a multidimensional message that outlined clear guidelines of leading a successful life in this world and in the Afterlife.

In fact, the guidance which the Holy Prophet (pbuh) brought was comprehensive and covered all aspects of our lives. He laid down a foundation, which are based on two principles:

I testify that there is no god except Allah and I testify that Muhammad is His Messenger

The *kalimah shahādah* is not a ritual phrase that makes a believer a practising Muslim. In contrast, the starting point is to declare the Oneness of Allah Who owns the world and mankind and their destiny; therefore, everyone is heading towards Him. Like the day and night, man should be to draw an important lesson about the dual principle of contrast: he has the free will to choose good and evil.

In our daily lives we encounter conflicting emotions which are innate to man's personality. We experience the highs and lows in life. By way of example, we cannot our anger which represents our base self. We want to hit back and take revenge. In light of our uncontrollable tendency, the Holy Prophet (pbuh) has warned us that "anger eats away *imān* just as fire eats away the straw or wood."

The response to this natural trait of man – anger – by religious leaders or faiths is either idealistic or irrational. Consider the Sermon on the Mount in which Prophet `Isā (pbuh) is believed to have said: "If anyone slaps you on the right cheek, present to him the left cheek also." This is the Christian attributed to the noble personality of `Isā (pbuh). As much as the teaching is sublime it goes against human nature. Forgiveness for such an action is the right thing to do; however, to give the other cheek contradicts the Qur'ānic teachings which are based on sound principles of man's inner temperaments.

Consider the following *āyah* to understand the Qur'ānic prescription of responding evil with good:

Good and evil are not of the same category. Always meet the challenge of evil with that which is good. When there is enmity between you and the other party, there is a possibility he will be like a close friend.

(41: 34)

Light and darkness are not of the same category. If one is faced with darkness then procure any source of light, even it is a matchstick. In this way darkness can be dispelled. Moreover, the Qur'ān urges us to cultivate the quality of *sabr* (patience) in its broadest sense and magnanimity (one who is fortunate).

Those who walk on the earth in humility are those who have goodwill to all. They are like the refreshing morning breeze causing the buds to smile into flowers, bringing fragrance, happiness and peace to mankind. That is the role of a Muslim. When they are confronted with ignorant people (*jāhils*) who hurl abuse at them they respond by saying *salām*. In essence, it a positive trait of a Muslim who does not indulge in wranglings and quarrels. Furthermore, when they are confronted with anything that is vain or worthless, they bypass that unpleasant situation with grace and dignity.

In the noble life of the Holy Prophet (pbuh) we see how he conducted himself under adverse circumstances. He did not harm or abuse anyone when he was persecuted or when he had to face an enemy in battles like Badr or Uhud. The enemies mobilised their huge armies to kill him so that the Islamic movement would be vanquished. Their expectations were foiled in these battlefields.

If we have a sincere love for Islam then we have to practise what Islam stands for. Our moral conduct should reflect the noble character of the Holy Prophet (pbuh) in order to earn Allah's pleasure. The starting point is to control one's ego, which has the potential to destroy all good. It must be remembered that the Islamic way of life is grounded on the highest spiritual ideals. It means to live for Allah alone by emulating the perfect character of the Holy Prophet (pbuh). He is the basic personality Islam and imān. You cannot approach Allah by bypassing the Holy Prophet (pbuh) and you cannot understand the Qur'ān by bypassing the Holy Prophet (pbuh). He is the only teacher and the source of all blessings in this world and in the Afterlife.

A word of caution: Islam is not merely ritualistic gymnastics or an exercise in sectarian differences of opinion. This is not Islam. Islam means intense love for the Holy Prophet (pbuh) which should manifest itself in your life. The Sahābah loved him and what was the consequence? They were changed from ordinary barbaric human beings into supermen, for whom the angels would come and bow. This is what the love of the Holy Prophet (pbuh) gave them.

In the words of ʿAllāmah Iqbal:

Take yourself to the feet of the Holy Prophet (pbuh), for he alone is all region – the whole religion! If you cannot become a true lover of him then all your prayers and deeds taken together make you an Abu Lahab and not a Muslim.

Muhammad (pbuh): The Prophet of Allah

The second part of *kalimah shahādah* deals with the Messengership of the Holy Prophet (pbuh). It is comprehensive in scope and has a direct bearing the status of the most beloved of Allah.

In some circles of Muslims that have downplayed the status of the Holy Prophet (pbuh) by regarding him as an elder brother. This inappropriate address or misconception stems from the person's limited perception and his inability to see beyond. It is like a person who scans the horizon from different positions of the mountain. The higher he climbs the greater is his vision of the horizon. This analogy also applies to the person with firm faith who understands the personality of the Holy Prophet (pbuh) from a different angle.

As opposed to the one who says that Holy Prophet (pbuh) Is a mere mortal like us, `Allāmah Iqbal states that the most beloved of Allah is incomparable with anyone before him because he possesses the following qualities:

- He is the possessor of knowledge of the path of guidance
- He is the seal of Prophethood
- He is the first and last in the personification of love
- He is the Qur'ān who so is the criterion (*furqān*) that sets right from wrong in the universe
- He enjoys the unrivalled status of *Yāsin* and *Tāhā* (names of immense love by Allah)

There are two aspects of the Holy Prophet's personality as described in the Qur'ān: cosmic and mundane (earthly).

The Qur'ān says:

And We have not sent you (Muhammad) except as a mercy to the worlds.

(21: 07)

He is a mercy for the entire cosmos.

Concerning the Holy Prophet's personality in the light of his humanness, The Qur'ān is explicit:

(O Prophet) proclaim 'I am a human being as you are.' (18: 110)

However, this distinction is meant to dispel any misconception of divinity that has been done as in the case of Prophet ʿIsā by Christianity. Thus, the connotation of the above verse is to emphasise the humanity of the Holy Prophet (pbuh) so that Muslims may not fall prey (in view of his miraculous powers) to think that he is 'god' in any sense of the word.

To illustrate this point: charcoal is pure carbon and diamond is pure carbon. It is only the frequency of the vibration of the molecules that makes them different. Likewise, is the status of the Holy Prophet (pbuh) as a human being. He is a human being but he is like diamond and we are like charcoal. Therefore, there is a huge difference in terms of his status and his cosmic personality. In several āyāt of the Qur'ān, Allah makes mention of the Messengers by name. However, He does not address the Holy Prophet by name even once in the Qur'ān. Allah wants to demonstrate the grandeur of the position of the Holy Prophet's (pbuh) and the special relation with Him.

Here Allah demonstrates that He loves the Holy Prophet (pbuh) intensely and He wants the Muslims to honour the Holy Prophet (pbuh). In addition, Muslims should show decorum by not raising their voices above his and address him in an appropriate way. The Qur'ānic instruction for Muslims in all circumstances is explicit:

O believers, do not raise your voices above the voice of the Holy Prophet and do not talk to him in the fashion that you talk among yourselves, otherwise all your virtues will be annulled and you perceive not.

(49: 2)

85

Consider the honorific title of *Yāsin* for the Holy Prophet (pbuh). Love has screens which cannot be penetrated by others. The meaning is a mystery between the Lover and the Beloved. We do not know the meaning but we realise that this endearing title is one of deep love. Not only is the Holy Prophet (pbuh) venerable and honourable, even the soil that he walked on becomes honourable. In sum, the Holy Prophet (pbuh) has been sent as a Mercy for the whole world.

O Prophet, We have not sent you but as a mercy for all the worlds (and in all the worlds).

(21: 107)

The Holy Prophet is a witness that the universe or Allah's creation is infinite as the Qur'ān says:

Say: If all the sea were ink for my Lord's words, the sea would indeed be exhausted before my Lords words are exhausted, even if we were to add to it sea upon sea.

(18: 109)

The personality of the Holy Prophet (pbuh) can be compared to a lamp. If we illumine a room with 5000-watts lamps, every one of us will lose balance of our minds. How much would have been the power of that light in his *Mi'rāj* journey? To reiterate: Yes, the Holy Prophet (pbuh) was a human being but he is diamond and we are charcoal. No human being can compare to him. Therefore, it is a disingenuous attempt to downplay the sublime status of the Mercy to the worlds. Imagine an ant trying to figure out how big the Himalayas are or the moth asking how big the sun is. This type of irrational mindset forget that the power of Allah is immeasurable compared to our finite knowledge of the universe.

Likewise, the very essence of *'ubudiyyah* – submissive devotion to Allah – means that human being knows what is going to happen tomorrow. In other words, this *'ubudiyyah* is the foundation of din (Islam) and the spiritual life of a believer. That is why the Holy

Prophet (pbuh) has forbidden Muslims to dabble in astrology or astrological predictions.

In sum, love for the Holy Prophet (pbuh) demands an unconditional emulation of his blessed personality which is the embodiment of moral excellence.

Surah Fātihah and the Concept of Khalifat Allah

Allah addresses the Holy Prophet (pbuh) to say to the believers:

Say, if you love Allah, then follow me, and Allah will make you His beloved.

(3: 31)

Allah is the Creator, the Ruler, the Fashioner, the Guide and He controls everything in the entire universe. So Majestic and Infinite and different is He from His creation, yet He loves us. He has created man in the best of form with the best constitution. In this light Allah's relationship with mankind is that of mercy and love. Allah introduces Himself with the attributes of love in the opening of the Qur'ān: the Most Beneficent, most Merciful.

As the Sustainer (*Rabb*) of the world, He reinforces His attributes of love and mercy. At the same time, he reminds mankind that He is the Mater of the Day of Judgement - a reminder that belief in the Afterlife is essential to understand the justice of Allah. Also, mankind will have to give an account for their actions in this world.

We are totally dependent on Allah's mercy and assistance: therefore, our `ibādah and praying for Allah's assistance in every circumstance should reflect our submission to Him. The Holy Prophet (pbuh) taught us that a Muslim should pray to Allah for the most ordinary things in life. But here Allah is teaching us to aspire for the highest goal, the straight path, which is personified by the Prophets (*Anbiyā*) as the highest rank. In the descending order is the rank of *Siddiqin* – those who are the upholders of divine truth in their lives. The third category represents the *Shuhadā* – those who sacrificed their lives for the sake of truth and out of love for Allah. The fourth rank order are the *Sālihin* – those who led righteous lives in compliance with the divine code of life.

The above ranks can only be achieved if Muslims transform themselves to become worthy companionship of the beloved of Allah. The heart is the entry point of transformation through which flows virtues emphasised in the Qur'ān and sunnah. Transformation therefore does not accommodate ritualistic practices because they are counterproductive to the ideals of *Khalifat Allah*.

Muslims are given the divine responsibility to be the bearers and witnesses to all mankind about the existence of Allah in all of His attributes and the moral and spiritual order which is Islam. We see the working of Allah's attributes though we have not seen the personality of Allah. Essentially, we bear witness (shahid) to what Allah does and this affirms our conviction (*yaqin*) in Islam as the universal guide for mankind.

Love for Allah through salāh, for example requires an alignment of the body, mind and soul. In the *hadith al-qudsi* we are told by Allah that when His servant proceeds towards Him in *nafl* (optional) prayer by leading a righteous life, then he reaches that highest stage when Allah makes him His beloved. His organs and limbs metaphorically are highlighted to suggest that whatever he does symbolises his love for Allah. Moreover, Allah awareness (*taqwā*) is his guiding light to act fully and completely within the ambit of the Qur'an and the Sunnah.

The convex lens is like our spiritual heart. Through the love of Allah, the convex lens's focus is increased by way of *dhikr-Allah* (remembrance of Allah) and gradually acquires radiation from Allah and absorbs it. In a similar vein, we are told to establish *salāh* to remember Allah. As love is reciprocal, Allah in his infinite mercy said to the Holy Prophet (pbuh) to teach us: "Tell my servants – if they walk one step towards Me, I will move ten steps towards them."

When man becomes *Khalifat Allah* he realises his potential status. Just like every seed grows out of a plan, man has the potential to become *Khalifat Allah*. To earn this title, he has to follow the Islamic guidance. In other words, the Islamic guidance is the model of the Holy Prophet's (pbuh) personality. He is the embodiment, par excellence of *Khalifat Allah*.

Islam is the treasure house of the blessings of Allah. It is an inexhaustible treasure house only if we follow the perfect model of conduct (*uswah al-hasanah*) of our beloved Prophet (pbuh). This is clearly expressed in the following āyah:

Indeed, the best model is the Holy Prophet. (33: 21)

Our Prophet (pbuh) was the personification of the true meaning of *Khalifat Allah* which was the amalgam of the perfect code of life – Islam.

However, we Muslims have become like a small worm that crawls in the underground channels and we think that we are doing good by leading this life of ignorance and heedlessness. We need to do soul-searching in order to understand and assimilate the meaning and message of *Khalifat Allah*.

The Qur'ānic View of Disunity

Allah is One and therefore the entire universe is because it One Creator. Therefore, this world is a moral order and because Allah is One, all mankind is one family.

The principle of unity permeates the entire fabric of Islam as a code of life. Sadly, Muslims remain

disunited because they have violated a command of the Qur'ān which clearly states:

And hold fast to the bond of unity (rope of Allah) and never be divided (into sects or groups).

(3: 103)

The command of unity is a universal principle and cannot be compromised. Several āyāt warn us of disunity as a major sin that invites the displeasure of Allah.

There are three important norms that make up the Islamic way of life: unity, justice and selfless service to Islam. Overall, unity cannot be maintained unless these values are prioritised.

First, justice in its broadest sense is emphasised. Muslims are reminded to be guided by the principle of justice in every dimension of their lives. Everything that is done is for the sake of Allah alone. This implies that the ego must be brought under control so that universal justice may be established. Justice must be meted out also to enemies if circumstances demand transparency and equity. Likewise, justice cannot be compromised for the sake of family motives or other vested interests.

Justice is the cornerstone of unity and allows for the Muslim society to grow and prosper without suffering the blight of disunity. Like *taqwā*, justice creates a healthy, progressive environment that is free from ego-bloated pleasures. There is no place for manipulation, nepotism or self-interest. In contrast, the focus is on gaining the pleasure of Allah and strengthening the bond of unity as a divine pursuit.

The following *āyah* reinforces the pivotal role justice plays in the social order that Islam envisages:

O believers, stand by justice in everything and every dimension of life. Stand by and be for this justice (not for the sake of any expediency, personal benefit or any other motive), but purely for the sake of Allah...

(4: 135)

It is the principle of justice that supports unity. Justice fosters a sense of truth, fairness and integrity. It does not discriminate relatives, friends and enemies. Justice allows one to be steadfast in advancing the cause of truth to please Allah whose attribute is ʿadl (just). In contrast one of the causes of disunity comes through the clash of egos. When these individual egos are projected, justice is compromised. As a result, the consequences are grave: distorting the truth, protecting the unjust and exploiting the vulnerable and innocent ones.

Selfless service is an important virtue that requires walking on the steep path (ʿaqabah). In the early years of Islam, it referred to the abolishment of slavery, which was widespread in Arabia. It was considered the highest virtue for the ummah. A priority of universal significance are charitable acts that include opening a hospital or assisting a person who is in financial difficulties. Those who practise and encourage compassion towards one another (marhamah) are praised for their social virtues. Consider the āyah that speaks about a believer possessing social virtues, who honour their promises and who are steadfast in their faith in Allah and who face every trial of their life with grace and dignity (2: 177). It also applies to people who possess dignity of personality who display in their everyday life the quality of selfless service.

In the lives of the Sahābah the following trait was evident: they would sacrifice everything that they could afford for the benefit of others even though it might cause them hardship. This was an act of unity that removed self-interest and worldly considerations. In one of the battles against the disbelievers a Sahābi was seriously wounded and there were others who too were wounded. A voice was heard: "I am thirsty. I am dying." The person carrying water rushed to assist him. However, another wounded person also cried out for water. The dying Sahābi motioned to the person to assist the other dying Sahābi. There was a third cry for help and here again the concern for this dying person was attended to. However, none of them survived to quench their thirst while they were in the throes of death. This is an inspirational lesson of self-sacrifice.

The tragic turn of events in Muslim history points out to the disastrous consequences of disunity. There were mighty Muslim empires that ruled major parts of the world; sadly, they were fragmented by political rivalries, resulting in their collapse and eventually surrendering to Western powers. The adage "united we stand, divided we fall" holds true for the ummah as well.

Message to the Muslim Youth

The youth are the integral component of society; therefore, their contribution to a vibrant Islamic society cannot be ignored. In this particular sense, an ideology has a value system but Islam goes beyond the confines of a man-made system because it is a *din* – a code of life.

The Qur'ān outlines its vision of an ideological community in the following *āyah:*

> *You are the best of community for mankind – to command of all that*
> *is good and forbid that is evil as the believers of Allah.*

(3: 10)

This universal concept of community does not discriminate on the basis of race or materialism consideration; rather, it promotes values that are of enduring benefit to mankind. It is a truism that the rise of Islam is the greatest miracle in history. Even European historians acknowledged the contributions of Islam to the civilisations of the world. Islam did not operate in a vacuum: the Abbasid and Ottoman caliphates showed the peaceful nature of conquests even when they were faced with the hostile Christian armies. The rise and fall of empires were a result of the rulers' indulgence in material pursuits and moving away from the spirit of *da'wah.* Furthermore, schools of thought were formed, highlighting their sectarian outlook. Sadly, these divisions were a far cry from the principle of *tawhīd* (unity) that welded Muslim communities from different regions and with different cultural temperaments.

In the sharp era of decline Muslims ignored the fact that Islam as a din encompasses economic and social policies and 'secular' activities, which are considered to be of no consequences. This mindset has confined Islam to the mosque and ritualistic practices are deemed as essentials. Again, this narrow definition of Islam has to led to a cleavage of thought and practice that even the value system is disregarded at the altar of sectarian theology. Ironically, the Muslim community which was raised on the basis of tawhid is the most divided community.

Muslims should remember that a foundation without a structure is collapsible. Likewise, the *shahādah* without moral and spiritual values does not make up Islam. It does not even bring out the Prophetic model that is our perfect guide in this world. It must be remembered that the shahadah is integral to the Muslim identity, personality and responsibilities. That is why a verbal affirmation is not sufficient; it has to be actionable in every facet of our lives.

Sidq – absolute truthfulness in thought, word and deed is the first principle of the *shahādah*. The second principle relates to *amānah* - trustworthiness. These qualities were impressed in the noble personality of the Holy Prophet (pbuh) who was called *sādiq al-amin* (truthful and trustworthy). Even the *mushriks* (polytheists) of Makkah who opposed him vouched for these outstanding qualities. Only then was he commissioned to invite the people to Allah. The third factor is the burning desire for everyone to lead a successful life. This aspiration allows the human personality to be transformed with positive qualities.

Over the course of time Islam has become a cult. For the Muslim youth this becomes a serious challenge. The age of youth is the age of innocence. Perversion grows as age grows. In other words, the youth become vulnerable to these conflicts and become confused about the true Islam. Consequently, the Muslim community becomes stagnant and loses its dynamism. This is in contrast to the life-enriching teachings of the Qur'ān and the sunnah of the Holy Prophet (pbuh). The Qur'ān declares a successful life in these words when the odds are stacked against the believer:

Do not lose heart against the heaviest trials and never be in a state of grief, for you are bound to succeed if you are believers!

(3: 139)

In the light of the above āyah it is only the power of *imān* that can sustain in turbulent times. What does it entail? Strict adherence to the teachings of the Holy Qur'ān and internalising human values that are intrinsic to our personality.

To the Muslim youth: the age of youth is the age of innocence. Perversion grows as age grows. However, the deteriorating situation witnessed in the Muslim world has created a crisis of confidence in the minds of the youth. The cultic status, so fashionable in Muslim societies has alienated them from appreciating Islam as progressive, dynamic and revolutionary. It is in the timeless message of the Holy Qur'ān and the perfect Prophetic model which are perennial sources of Islam.

Muslims need to rediscover the whole of Islam for the harmonious blending of all values and dimensions of life. Islam believes that the gradation of values has to be accepted in all facets of life. In a similar manner Muslims cannot lead an isolated life nor live in a vacuum. For the youth who are the leaders of tomorrow they have to build a worldview in which the holistic teachings of the Qur'ān and the sunnah are brought out.

For the youth the message is emphatic: the world belongs to only those who are courageous and who do not believe in escapism.

Westernised Muslims

Muslims all over the world are faced with the problem of readjustment to the environment. There are clear-cut solutions to the challenges Muslims face, keeping in mind that they are inheritors of a glorious civilisation. However, they are unable to lead the world due to their passive response to the new world order that requires clarity of vision and maturity of goals.

The *dunyā* (world) is termed *dār al-'amal* (house of action) which eradicates all forms of superstition, ritualism and sectarian bickering. It would mean that the Muslim community would bring out the true spirit of *imān billah* (faith in Allah) in all facets of life. Furthermore, the spiritual orientation would be aligned according to the noble teachings of the Holy Prophet (pbuh). This is clearly set out in the following *āyah*:

> *It is not possible for a true believer, male or female, to have their own freedom of choice after they have been given a command by Allah and His Prophet.*

> (33: 36)

Essentially, the divine guidance states clearly that salvation is not based on ritualism, superstition or theological bickering which are common weaknesses in the Muslim community. It is the transformation of the human personality operating in a social order sanctioned by Allah that guarantees success in this world and in the Afterlife. The crisis of moral character has weakened our faith in Allah and His Attributes with the result that we do not posses the qualities expected of a true believer. This lamentable situation is noticeable in our poor grasp of *iqrā* paradigm – the blending of knowledge on the basis of faith (*yaqin*) and Allah-awareness (*taqwā*).

It must be remembered that Islam means discipline and not a signboard devoid of moral teachings. It is like a shop without merchandise! This mindset has eroded the Qur'ānic values which have no place for hypocrisy, vanity and self-interest. In fact, Muslims are reminded about the hostilities that Islam as a fledgling community experienced in Makkah; however, their resolve did not weaken nor did their *imān* show signs of decline. They were a determined community ready to sacrifice their wealth and lives to the cause of Islam. Compare their commitment to our fluctuating loyalty to Islam. In a short span of time this small group of Muslims brought the world under their sway and a force to be reckoned with. They represented the ideal of this *āyah:*

Honour belongs to Allah and His Prophet and the believers. (63: 8)

In our context, only those who possess a dynamic, loving and vibrant faith in Allah will deserve this honourable position. Unfortunately, we have reached rock bottom of our degradation that the Zionist entity has forcibly taken control of first *qibla* – Masjid Al-Aqsa which is ironically surrounded by weak Arab countries. (The genocide and ethnic cleansing of Gaza by the Zionist aggressors is a grim reminder of the apathy and impotence of the Arab regimes and Muslim countries). As an admonition the Qur'an addresses the believers, individually and collectively:

Whoever revolts against the forces of evil and establishes his loyalty towards Allah, he obtains a support which will never fail him. (2: 256)

In this context Muslims are reminded that Islam is the alchemy that transforms all base metals into gold, and it has proved itself to be the alchemy. It was sent by Allah to the most backward people – the Arabs of those days. They challenged the whole world of *bātil* (of all that was false) and they conquered the world and established the truth!

It is a truism that Muslims living as a minority community are tied up with the challenges of Western civilisation. But this not unique to South African Muslims as Muslim-majority countries are also Westernised; sadly, they are leaving their centuries-old culture and embracing modernism. There is a theory of historical compulsion which states that countries (in this case Muslim countries) are not immune from the influence of other countries or civilisations that are superior in their worldview. These Muslim countries surrender completely because they are passive and share no idealism. As a matter of fact, the caravan of humanity moves all the time leaving these reactive communities to be trampled under a superior civilisation.

Muslims have not fully implemented the mission of Islam because they are no longer inspired by the Islamic idealism. The reasons are obvious: indulging in un-Islamic practices and not following the *uswah al-hasanah* (excellent model). Additionally, the incursion of colonialism in Asia and Africa also came with a missionary agenda to de-Islamise the Muslims. The repercussions of this colonial project has had a lasting impact on Muslim countries which have not shed completely Western influences on their educational and political systems.

Islam has a set of values which makes it a universal religion. If these values are ignored or neglected then the outward forms of Islam become dominant. This is clearly evident when the so-called Islamic attire is worn in foreign countries as a mark of piety. It is important to take note that a measure of a person's *imān* is his moral integrity and his conduct. From this positive attitude flows the purity of intention that makes up the spiritual dimensions of Islam. It is the moral life rather than the perceived external appearance of a Muslims that can be practised in any part of the world.

Islam can adjust anywhere because it is anchored on positive ideals that are universal in character and application. This is clearly outlined in the following *āyah:*

> *You are the best ideological group which has been raised and chosen by Allah for the purpose that you will establish all that is good and eradicate all that is evil, as believers in Allah.*

(3: 110)

Muslims are expected to follow Islam in it totality; otherwise, Islam will become a cult with an otherworldly orientation combined with a few ethical principles. In other words, Islam will lose its dynamic character and universal appeal and *da'wah*-oriented mission.

Tasawwuf: Spiritual Pursuit in Islam

Tasawwuf in the recent past has evoke two different reactions by scholars of Islam. On the one hand it is discredited as a foreign element that has no relevance to Islam and on the other it has been overstrained with practices that are also alien to Islamic teachings. Worse are the practitioners, the so-called spiritual guides who have distorted *tasawwuf* that it becomes difficult to even recognise the essential forms that make up the inner dimensions of Islam.

The Qur'ān explicitly states the function of the Holy Prophet (pbuh) in these words:

It is He Who has sent among the unlettered nation a Messenger from among themselves, who communicates the message as it comes to him from Almighty Allah. He purifies them and he expounds the Qur'ān and he teaches wisdom.

(62: 2)

Here Allah defines the functions for which the Holy Prophet (pbuh) was sent:

- He gives the people the Law or the divine code of life.
- He purifies those that accept the message. Therefore, the process of purification is different from learning the shari`ah.
- He teaches the Qur'ān (*Kitāb*) and
- He teaches the wisdom.

How to be a Muslim is derived from the shari`ah which guides one to be a true believer. The graded status of *tasawwuf* has its roots in the Qur'ān and the sunnah. The terms used are meant to give this discipline a structured form without deviating from the spirit of the sunnah.

Consider the term *tariqah*. It is the path or the way that provides a blueprint to earn Allah's pleasure. Thus, the methodology employed is the *tariqah:* developing the human personality from the lower level to the higher level. There is perseverance to fight against the impulses of *nafs al-ammārah* (base self), to nurture the soul to be in obedience to the shari`ah by consciously following a methodology for which earn divine reward and Divine pleasure are promised.

The next level is to develop *ma`rifah:* Godly knowledge beyond which is that 'superior' knowledge called `*irfān.* It has three levels:

- Man should know himself. He should nurture his personality as a Muslim and adopt the methodology that will give him access about himself -`*ilm al-nafs.*
- `*Ilm al-Āfāq* – knowledge about the environment and the cosmos.
- Knowledge about Allah, to know Allah and experience and build *yaqin* (conviction) in the fullest sense.

In the celebrated works of classical Sufis, *tasawwuf* has a common theme: cleansing the soul (*tazkiyah*) in compliance with the shari`ah. These works refute the deviant interpretations of those who are not grounded in the inner dimensions of this tradition. Focused spiritual training under an experienced master leads to the path of *ma`rifah* and `*irfān* -the core spirit of *tasawwuf.* Essentially, shari`ah is the foundation on which the structure of *tasawwuf* is built.

In the words of Shaykh Abdul Qādir Jilāni:

The spiritual pilgrim cannot go one hair's breath out of the shari`ah. This is tasawwuf.

Tasawwuf in its pristine form (shari`ah-compliant) had to counteract over the centuries the negative influence of mysticism which was introduced by misguided Sufis. It is therefore understandable when the *mashāi'kh* strove tirelessly to purge these syncretic practices that had tarnished the reputation of *tasawwuf.* Likewise, those who are caught up in a web of theological bickering and ignore the higher objectives of the shari`ah fit into the category of the following āyah:

The example of those who learn the Torah (but could not assimilate it for a transformation of their personalities) is like a donkey carrying a load of books.

(62: 5)

In sum, *tasawwuf* assimilates the inner dimensions of Islam and represents a quest leading to the path of *ma`rifah.*

Materialism: a Challenge to World Religions

It is clearly evident that the world in general and religions in particular are confronted with an existential crisis in terms of upholding moral values. Truth, justice and beauty have become hollow terms considering the invasion of countries in the twentieth century by superpowers and occupiers (The settler colonisers like Zionist Israel of Palestine are a grim reminder).

Countries have also been exposed to atheistic ideologies like communism and have trampled on universal values that promote justice, equality and brotherhood. In communism materialism is the centrepiece of economic and social exploitation; the tragic consequences of tyranny and dictatorship are writings on the wall.

In Islam the universal concept of brotherhood is founded on the belief that mankind as an organic unity represents an honourable position. The Qur'ān says:

Verily, We (Allah) has honoured the children of Adam.   (17: 70)

Dignity of the human being requires respect and honour. The real test of dignity is the promotion of goodness and eradicating the culture of jealousy, hatred and contempt for the others. This is stark contrast to communism where a godless society has the choice to do away with moral values. Likewise, religions should foster a culture of godliness rather than focusing on salvation as a counter response to the epidemic of capitalism. Materialism creates a consumer society where obsession for worldly desires is given priority. And the emergence of a permissive society which is shorn of moral values is a bitter reality.

Communism and materialism create an illusion of a just society based on their respective ideologies. In a broader context both these systems have failed dismally in addressing the plight of mankind. Instead, they have created a cadre of elites who have a common mindset - exploitation. Obviously, there is no moral bond of unity between human beings and the last century has witnessed an erosion of universal values like truth, social justice, righteousness and integrity. In fact, communism created a bloody reign of terror in its relentless pursuit of addressing social injustice. In a similar vein, materialism has entrenched the culture of a capitalistic economy which disregards a welfare society.

In Islam a social order highlights the moral bond of unity among human beings. Universal values like justice, equality, honesty deepen one's respect for others. Therefore, there is no place for lip service for religious identity politics which takes away mankind from establishing a real bond with the Creator of the universe. Therefore, there is genuine need to return to Allah and Muslims can take the lead to demonstrate the following qualities in their lives:

- You cannot be godly if you are selfish.
- If you love Allah, love human beings.
- Practise the message of the Holy Prophet (pbuh): All creation is Allah's family.
- Deal every human being firstly as a human being and not as a Muslim, Christian etc.
- Appreciate good wherever it is to be found even if it is your enemy. Hate the evil not the evildoer.

This is the Islamic principle of goodwill for all mankind. It is not a theoretical principle enshrined in Constitutions but was fully implemented by the Holy Prophet (pbuh) in his interaction with different tribes and with his enemies too. At the conquest of Makkah, the Holy Prophet (pbuh) forgave his enemies who had persecuted him by echoing the words of Prophet Yusuf (peace be upon him) to his cruel brothers:

There will be no punishment inflicted on you this day. May Allah forgive your sins for He is the Most Merciful.

(12: 92)

It was a an appeal for mercy because the enemies knew that the Holy Prophet (pbuh) was the personification of love and mercy. Furthermore, the Holy Prophet (pbuh) the same principle in word and deed, and commanded in the words of the Holy Qur'ān:

Repel evil with good. (23: 96)

Muslims are reminded to develop a culture of moral integrity in all circumstances and situations. Presently, humanity is undergoing crises that calls for a return to the universal values which Islam proclaims as truth, justice and beauty. This Islamic ideal has been relegated to the margins and instead a code of expediency has been adopted. Essentially, expediency is self-centred and cannot provide social stability.

Therefore, the message to the Muslims and all the rest of humanity is: *Return to Allah genuinely.* And obtain from Him the light to dispel the darkness. Otherwise, this darkness will continue and consume wherever you will find it. Materialism has spread its tentacles all over, covering every facet of human life. Perhaps it is not too late; so let us act now; otherwise it will be too late.

Women in Islam

Women occupy an honourable position in Islam and have shari`ah guarantees in terms of financial independence. Compare her dignified life ensured by Islam to her enslavement in past civilisations to appreciate her dominant role in a Muslim society. In pre-Islamic Arabia she was considered a chattel and looked upon with contempt. In contrast Islam brought about a revolutionary change in her status that is unrivalled to the present day.

Equality of opportunities with specific roles assigned to males and females is best expressed in marriage. This means that their biological functions determine their respective roles in society. That man enjoys a degree higher than woman implies that by virtue of his biological disposition he is able to carry out responsibilities in carrying out responsibilities for his family. More importantly, he is able to bear challenging tasks that women cannot perform. Therefore, as a husband he is regarded as the guardian of family life.

The first principle of Islamic social life is that all affairs are conducted by mutual consultation. In the case of marriage, the husband may not dictate terms that are in conflict with the concept of *shurā* (mutual consultation). His wife is his life partner and therefore has an equal legal status in maintaining a harmonious family relationship.

Paradise lies under the feet of the mother brings out the significant role of women. Imagine the goal of a healthy, vibrant family life can only be achieved through deep respect for a mother. In order of importance her function in Muslim society is vital. A society may slip into wickedness or lose its moral bearing if the woman goes astray due to particular influences. Overall, a child can be raised in a warm, nurturing environment by a woman who has strong moral values. She is thus a fortress of goodness and can withstand the forces of evil and corruption.

In the name of liberty, equality and fraternity promoted by the Renaissance, the traditional role of women underwent a radical change. The emancipation of women changed the boundaries of gender relations and as a result created a dysfunctional family life. Marriage was preceded by romance and courtship; premarital relationship was considered a norm to determine compatibility between the prospective couple. In sum, the 'marriage made in heaven' slogan was a charade that brought out grim realities of frustration, bitterness and instability.

This culture of equality was a sham and eroded values of trust, mutual respect and dignity in the Victorian era. Instead, women suffered greatly in the name of emancipation. This is reflected in their dual role of being an employee and a housewife at the same time. In Islam this extra burden to supplement an income by the wife is not encouraged unless certain conditions are met. In the same strain, intermingling of the sexes in the workplace considered acceptable in the West is frowned upon by Islam.

Marriage according to Islam is an act of worship ('ibādah) and impresses on the following qualities: dignity, chastity and mutual respect.

In an address at the University of Ottawa in Canada, the author (Dr Ansari) had the following conversation with a lady regarding the position of women in Islam.

After I answered the question, she bluntly retorted: "What do you say about the purdah system?"

"Purdah is not compulsory in the manner in which it is being practised in India. However, it is preferable or better than the rules of conduct you are observing in your country," I replied.

She said: "How can you defend the purdah! You are a doctor of philosophy! How can you speak like this?"

I said: "My good lady, God is the creative force in the universe, He is hidden behind the purdah (screen). The woman is the creative force in human society. Should she rather imitate God or the devil that goes about naked!" I continued, "If you have a pebble of no value, would you place it in a safe?" She said, "No!"

I said: "If you have a diamond, would you have it lying around or will you keep it in a safe?"

She said: "Yes!"

I replied: "The Islamic culture regards woman as diamonds and your culture regards woman as pebbles and stones."

Discipline in Dhikr

Islam is a religion of discipline and is not based on dogmatic beliefs, superstitions or irrational system of salvation. On the contrary, Islam is firmly rooted in clear belief (`aqā'id) as elucidated in the Qur'ān.

> *It is not possible for the believers whether male or female, when given a command by Allah or His Messenger, to have any choice in the matter.*
>
> (33: 36)

It is the spirit of obedience that pervades the life of a believer. Whatever action he performs is guided by the Prophetic statement: with genuine *imān* and self-introspection (*ihtisāb*).

In our *salāh*, for example, we need to develop Allah-awareness and to examine our actions. Likewise, a person speaking the truth, expecting praises from people has lost the true value of it. It implies that he has an ulterior motive and his action is not done to please Allah. Therefore, it is important that our actions are infused with spirituality (*ruhāniyah*) by embedding the quality of *ihtisāb* in our lives.

There is a general tendency by many Muslims who have no real understanding of *tasawwuf* that spirituality which resembles mysticism does not require acts of worship. In other words, they are neglectful of salāh and focus on good deeds only. This behaviour or mindset disrupts the equilibrium and discipline emphasised by the Islamic teachings.

On the contrary, many Muslims pray, fast and love Allah and the Holy prophet (pbuh) but they have forgotten that discipline is the condition which will make them good and great. Consequently, it was impossible for any of the Sahābah to disobey the Holy Prophet (pbuh) even if they had to risk their lives. Whatever he commanded, was carried out without question. That obedience which the Holy Prophet (pbuh) advised was demonstrated wholeheartedly and gladly accepted.

Compare the Sahābah's implicit faith and obedience to the Holy Prophet (pbuh) to the state of affairs in the Muslim community. Sectarian differences have reached alarming levels that even the mosques are built along these lines. Worse still, these places of 'ibādah have become the battle ground for entrenching a sectarian position. Keeping in mind that salāh instils the quality of humility and seeking forgiveness from Allah, how is then possible to build a community life in accordance with the teachings of the Qur'ān and the sunnah?

Discipline in the early years of Islamic conquest is best illustrated by the unflinching loyalty of Sayyidinā Khālid bin Walid. In the midst of the battle as a general he was informed by Sayyidinā 'Umar to hand over the command of the army over to his subordinate. This demotion did not sway his emotions or harbour any grievance against the command of the second Khalifa. He fought valiantly as an ordinary soldier for the pleasure of Allah.

Discipline forms the bedrock of fulfilling our pledges and practising constancy in our 'ibādah. In our dhikr schedule it is strongly advised that a routine that allows for ease and convenience be followed. Dhikr should commence with a minimum quantity by building an ethos of constancy (istiqāmat). Thereafter, it should be gradually increased to suit the capacity and temperament of the individual. Allah demands from us a health and sound spiritual heart that is free from the burdens of excessive dhikr. In the words of the Qur'ān:

And He has not laid upon you any hardship in the din. (22: 78)

Salāh (Devotional Prayer)

Muslims believe and practise the five pillars of Islam among which salāh is performed daily. These are the foundations of Islam and therefore are emphasised in the Qur'ān and hadith literature. Moreover, the foundation has to be solidified through other acts of Islamic teachings so that the structure may be strong and of an excellent quality.

Many Muslims have a superficial understanding of the vision and mission of Islam and are inclined to confine themselves to a ritualistic practice of the five pillars of Islam. As a result, they lack the true essence and meaning of 'ibādah and make no effort apply the whole of Islam in their lives. In the case of salāh, their performance resembles gymnastics which is devoid of that special, intimate communion between the 'abd (sincere servant) and his Lord, Allah. It is a sublime communion that is animated with love, submission and obedience. Overall, it is the spirit that permeates the quality of salāh rather than ritualistic postures.

The Holy Prophet (pbuh) by his noble examples taught Muslims the etiquettes of salāh. First, they should run to the musjid in order to join the salāh in progress. There should be decorum (adab) in the state of salāh and the postures should reflect a sense of humility. The Holy Prophet (pbuh) shortened prayers in congregation (jamā'ah) and lengthened them in his solitary hours. He gave due consideration to minors, elders and the vulnerable people.

The Holy Prophet (pbuh) said that salāh as an 'ibādah should reflect a devotional attitude as explained in the hadith in these words:

Worship your Lord as if you are seeing Him. If this is not possible for you. (the lowest mode of worship is that you) are conscious that Allah is seeing you and you are worshipping Him.

When we offer salāh, we are easily distracted by stray thoughts and on many occasions, we are overpowered by worldly matters that we tend to forget that we are expected to be in communion with Allah. It is therefore not surprising that we utter the words of prayer, but our minds are somewhere else.

It must be remembered that Allah is the Creator, Ruler of the entire universe; He is *samad*: He is in no need of anything that He created. Everything is dependent on Him and He is independent of everything. Yet out of love for us Allah is inviting us through the adhān to His divine audience. What greater honour can there be for Muslims. As the *Khalifat Allah* we are commanded to imbue ourselves with divine qualities.

The spiritual relationship between the `abd and Allah is beautifully illustrated in this analogy:

When the iron filings come into contact with the magnet, they are magnetised. If they don't come into contact with the magnet, they remain iron filings, but when they are magnetised, they don't become the magnet. When the servant of Allah approaches Him with the same spirit of love, as the Qur'ān says:

The believers are strong in their love for Allah. (2: 165)

Thus, through salāh one becomes magnetised.

The Holy Qur'ān also admonishes the believers who put on a display of piety in their salāh:

Cursed are those who pray, who are absent in their prayers. Those who want only to be seen and praised and refuse to assist people.
(107: 4-7)

The postures of salāh are intertwined with the spirit of humility; therefore, it has to be performed with serenity, composure and a state of consciousness. All in all, there must be the presence of the heart (*hudhur al-qalb*).

Imagine the sublime position of the Holy Prophet (pbuh) even in our salāh! The *tahiyyāt* is an affirmation (*shahādah*) that the Holy Prophet (pbuh) is the gateway to obtain Allah's blessings. Moreover, we are reminded that he is Allah's `abd and Messenger. Then through a sense of gratitude we are reminded about the illustrious Prophet Ibrāhim (peace upon him) through whom guidance came to us and perfected in the noble personality of our Holy Prophet (pbuh).

The salāh also contains a *du'ā* of seeking Allah's forgiveness for our shortcomings as we are all fallible human beings.

112

The salāh also contains a *du'ā* of seeking Allah's forgiveness for our shortcomings as we are all fallible human beings.

What is Islam

Dr Ansari laments the fact that as one of the soldiers of Islam he has contend against anti-Islamic forces all over the world. In addition, he has to face Muslim ignorance, apathy and intern al bickering over trivial issues while the enemies of Islam are challenging in their devious ways the very fundamentals of Islam.

Sadly, the youth are gravitating towards materialism while many are leaving the fold of Islam. Again, Muslim scholars in general are to be blamed because they do not offer a structured, coherent presentation of Islam that is compatible with the temperament and aspirations of the youth. Consequently, the moral values that Islam emphasise are lost in the maze of ritualistic practices. Unlike Christianity and Hinduism where religious beliefs and doctrines are enshrouded in mystery, Islam is anchored on the pristine teachings of the Qur'ān and the sunnah.

Islam was born in the broad daylight of history and sustained over the centuries with an unbroken link to the Prophetic era. In this way the Muslims took the greatest care in preserving the historical character of Islam which is free from misinterpretation and manipulation of its primary sources. Compare the philosophies of Hinduism, Buddhism and Zoroastrianism and there is a common theme in their worldview: the salvation of mankind consists of renouncing the world and pursuing the path of mysticism.

By contrast the foundations of Western civilisation are materialistic in nature, hedonistic (seeking sensual pleasure) in outlook, utilitarian (for material advancement) in worldview and its civilisation is based on expediency. Islam in its completeness maintains a balance that is aimed at developing the human personality. It encompasses the definition of being a Muslim of the following āyah:

And all that is in the heavens and the earth are Muslim. (3: 383)

Islam requires mankind to follow the natural laws termed as divinely-revealed laws for the betterment of mankind. It shuns formal piety as it breeds rigidity and arrogance; likewise, it gives an orientation that *"wherever you turn, Allah is there." (2: 115)* The Qur'ān expands the concept of *righteousness* which includes spending one's wealth for the sake of Allah to family in distress, orphans and the needy followed by establishing salāh and giving out zakāh. Altruism or selfless sacrifice is given priority in this verse.

Social ethics or obligations were emphasised even in Muslims' dealing with the disbelievers. The incident of the Sahābi, Sayyidinā Hudhaifa is illustrative. He left Makkah on the undertaking to the Quraysh that he would not join the army of the Muslims against them. He related this incident to the Holy Prophet (pbuh) when he arrived in Madinah. When the battle of Badr of imminent the Muslim army comprised 313 poorly-equipped soldiers. Sayyidinā Hudhaifa came to join the army but the Holy Prophet (pbuh) forbade him on account of the undertaking he made with the Quraysh. The battle of Badr had taken place after a lapse of time when Sayyidinā Hudhaifa left Makkah. For the Prophet of Allah, a promise should not be broken even in adverse circumstances.

Again, the Holy Qur'ān reminds the believers that truth, justice and other virtues that make up social ethics should not be abandoned at the altar of expediency:

Those who stick to perseverance and patience when in hardship and losses
(2: 177)

In the Qur'ānic terminology, the *Sābirin* are those who cultivate and practise sabr in its broadest sense when they are faced with calamities and trusting their complete faith in Allah say: *"Everything belongs to Allah and to Him we must return." (2: 155-6)* In other words, their reliance keep their faith stronger and therefore are able to face challenges with courage and dignity.

This life-enriching lesson bolsters a person's conviction (*yaqin*) in Allah and prepares to trust Allah in every circumstance. Otherwise, pessimism sets in and a believer in his ignore and weak faith laments with indignation to Allah! This behaviour implies that he is in a loser in this world and in the Afterlife.

The Qur'ān is explicit in its proclamation that those who uphold and practise the various dimensions of social ethics, *"they alone are truthful.*" (2: 177) and possess the sterling qualities of a refined and noble character.

These believers in their proclamation are the ones that are truthful to Allah and His Prophet (pbuh).

Our Concept of Islam

The problems Muslims face in South Africa are no different from the theological bickering in Pakistan. These differences have their root in rigidity and a kufr-bashing tendency. The `ulama of the classical era of Islam possessed higher ideals and maintained a culture of decorum (*adab*) in their differing positions on peripheral issues of *fiqh* (jurisprudence).

Islam has a value system on which the foundation of Islam is built. From it emerges a system of norms, then principles (*maqāsid*) through which laws (*ahkām*) are formulated. This holistic approach has been discarded by Muslims who approach it from a partial, historical, cultural or philosophical perspective. It is therefore unsurprising when a pietist and ritualistic practice of Islam is visible.

For example, salāh consists of physical postures which are prescribed as explained by the Holy Prophet (pbuh). However, it needs to be infused with a true spirit because we are in communion with Allah. Salāh has to be offered five times a day within a specified time so that the remembrance of Allah is maintained. At the same time, salāh is mandatory for a Muslim and is therefore non-negotiable. It must however not create a piety complex that will be used to look down upon others or behaving differently from them. The ideal of Islam is comprehensive in its scope as decribed in these words:

O believers! Enter into Islam completely and comprehensively. (2: 208)

In the light of the above *āyah* the entire worldview of shari`ah is based on the concept of progress and evolution. In the same vein our `ibādah, salāh and fasting, for example, will have that force and spirit that bring us closer in sincerity to Allah. The calculator mentality of obtaining reward (*thawāb*) will be of secondary importance.

There are two forces challenging the world of Islam: conservatism and modernism. The general tendency is to conserve everything that has come from their forefathers through a rigid interpretation of the Islamic teachings believing that 'all that is old is good.' The other force – modernism is becoming very dangerous and in its wake created an inferiority complex among Muslims. The modernist Muslims believe that the Western nations are making progress in terms of science and technology and are far superior to the Muslim nations who lag behind in these sciences. For them material progress is the benchmark of success and prosperity.

A balance between these extremes is progressive orthodoxy which steers away from the rigidity of conservatism and creates an Islamic ethos that regards knowledge in a holistic sense. This outlook is line with the *iqrā* paradigm revealed to the Holy Prophet (pbuh).

Another disturbing trend of the modernist Muslims is the intellectual dishonesty of their attitude towards the Islamic teachings. They are so overwhelmed by the West that they attempt to give an apologetic interpretation of the Qur'ānic ideals to suit their inferiority complex. Against this bleak background an effort has to made to create a powerful movement in the world of Islam which can rejuvenate the spirit of Islam.

The starting point (for this renaissance) is to develop a living and dynamic relationship with Allah, to experience Him – this is the very foundation of Islam. Without building up that consciousness and experience of God, you will not be able to build up that ideal according to the Islamic foundation. When we proceed on this road of building up our consciousness of God then certain things are bound to appear in the character of that man or woman. The first fruit is humility: the more a person experiences God, the more humble he/ she becomes. They do not compromise on truth but are inspired with the ideal to make others happy.

Humility accompanied by the pursuit of the higher goals in Islam is a counterbalance to trivial issues and a narrow, rigid interpretation of the Islamic teachings.

Allah is the source of all Wisdom, all Truth, Power and Wisdom and therefore a believer has to strengthen this bond with Allah through humility, gentleness, selflessness, integrity etc. These qualities create a culture of godliness (*taqwā*) that ensures happiness in this world and in the Afterlife. Muslims are exhorted to follow these ideals because in the Prophetic words we are reminded to "work for the ideals of Islam as you are going to die tomorrow."

Again, Muslims are reminded not to procrastinate in achieving these ideals otherwise they will relapse into a state of moral and spiritual inertia. The light of Islam and the greatness and glory which Islam brings are captured in this āyah:

Whoever strives in Our way, We will make the path smooth for him – and lead him to the goal.

(29: 69)

Attainment of Holiness

This is the Book, in it is guidance, without doubt, to those who fear Allah.
(2: 1-2)

Keeping in mind the above āyah, the prevalent Muslim predicament can only be addressed if the Muslim community can adopt a two-fold approach. First, they must build a positive thinking, and second, they must make a positive contribution to the whole of mankind.

When Muslims aspire for higher ideals then the minor issues are of no consequence. If, however, Muslims persist in dwelling on minor issues then they are like the ones scratching in the gutter to see how much dirt there is.

Muslims should remember a bitter fact that shorn of higher Islamic ideals and spiritual values they will in their vulnerability visit charlatans like fake spiritual advice for guidance. Likewise, Muslims who are inclined to read avidly Western literature will not seek advice from enlightened ʿulama. This cleavage is a dangerous trend as its sets apart the Muslim community from accessing the pristine teachings from the Qur'ān and the sunnah.

Central to our lives is the *uswah al hasanah* that is the model of excellence. Muslim attachment to the noble personality of our Holy Prophet (pbuh) is not formal nor is it ritualistic. His exemplary life should be our primary because it exemplifies his guidance for humanity. The Prophet (pbuh) was devoted to the service of others that even his bitter enemies regarded him as the most truthful and trustworthy (*As-Sādiq al-Amin*). For Muslims, the code of life is divinely sanctioned and anchored on the *uswah al-hasanah*.

In Islam, Allah wants his ʿabd to cultivate a personal relationship with Him, not a distant God who is aloof from His creation. For the youth who are disillusioned with the formalities preached by a certain segment of the ʿulama fraternity, faith in Allah (*Imān Billāh*) should be emphasised. This positive mindset will help them understand the true meaning and message of the *kalima shahadah*. Moreover, it facilitates another dimension *of jihād fi sabillilāh*: it is striving in God, to acquire direct experience of God, and it is for this experience that Islam came. To this end, prayer and fasting as well as other Islamic obligations should create a deep-rooted presence that Allah is aware of all our actions and these should bring us closer to Him.

The miracle of transformation by the Holy Prophet (pbuh) to the Sahābah was a divine function in the form of *tazkiyah: "to rehearse to them His Signs, to purify them."* The Holy Prophet (pbuh) is the basis of Islam and the dynamo of his personality will continue to change us with godliness and holiness. In fact, the trajectory of transformation of our character and personality only takes place through a living and genuine commitment to him.

The Holy Prophet (pbuh) has been commissioned for the purpose of *tazkiyah* and this is the goal of Islam – the transformation of the personality. Rituals are only a means to an end. Likewise, the moral laws are not the goal, but means to an end. The goal is the attainment of holiness and to come into contact with Allah, for He is All Holy. The holiness that is to be acquired is conferred through the dynamic personality of the Holy Prophet (pbuh). As the Qur'ān confirms that the Holy Prophet (pbuh) will continue to perform this function which performed for his Companions and all those of the Muslims until the day of Qiyāmah.

It is important for the youth to reconnect with the Qur'ān and the sunnah so that they may walk the path of Islam with greater enthusiasm. At the same time, they should rediscover the dynamic and progressive interpretation of Islam as a legacy that is inscribed in the lives of the pious predecessors (*salaf al-sālih*).

Murid (Initiation)

The *bay'ah* (pledge) is given to Allah. The aspirant (*sālik*) wants to reform his spiritual life in accordance with the teachings of Islam under the supervision of a spiritual guide (murshid). This hid āyah (guidance) in the *tasawwuf* terminology flows from Allah through the Holy Prophet (pbuh) and from him through the chain (*silsilah*) of sufi luminaries up to the present day.

A prerequisite for a person who wants to acquire spiritual refinement (*ihsān*) is to take care of his five daily prayers (salāh). These should be read with concentration, enthusiasm and contemplation. The prayer should be imbued with the spirit of communion with Allah and with a vibrant consciousness. The presence of heart (*hudhur al-qalb*) allows for a seamless communion with Allah.

The *murid* (aspirant) should not be overenthusiastic in performing extra optional prayers (*nawāfil*) in his initial stages of his spiritual journey. Rather, he should that the inner dimensions of prayer are reinforced and consistency is maintained. Additionally, it must be offered with the fullest spiritual fervour and in a state of mind where one does not see it as a burden. It is the love for Allah that should permeate all the facets of 'ibādah. Moreover, the goal of being a *murid* is to be immersed in divine pleasure (*ridā ilāhi*).

Dhikr is rooted in the sunnah of the Holy Prophet (pbuh) and generates a spirit of self-sacrifice. Consider the following *āyah* which sets out a clear message about the sunnah-in-action:

> *You are not performing real virtue until and unless you sacrifice for the sake of Allah that which you love most.*

> (3: 92)

Real virtue (*birr*), for example, is responding with a forgiving smile to a person who abuses you rather than becoming enraged and yielding to your lower self (*nafs al-ammārah*). Without doubt, our human inclinations, temperaments can be a barrier to attaining levels of spirituality. Likewise, *dhikr* is the powerhouse of maintaining an equilibrium (*i'tidāl*) and composure that exemplifies the adage of 'a sound mind lives in a sound body.'

In this spiritual journey the test of true faith begins with challenges that are meant to develop a righteous life. Trials of different kinds require steadfastness (*istiqāmat*) that brings one closer to Allah. If you are walking the way of truth then Allah will take care of you in all circumstances:

Those who proclaim that Allah is their Lord and they remain steadfast, the angels of Allah come to them with the message: "Be not afraid of anything nor grieve, for your reward will be jannah which you have been promised."

(41: 30)

Islamic Value System

The youth are the backbone of any society and with them rest the future of Islam too.

Keeping in mind the panorama of events Muslims face today, the past particularly the last two centuries cannot be forgotten. In fact, the nineteenth and twentieth centuries marked a sharp decline in Muslim fortunes in every facet of life. The intrusion of the political hegemony of the West over Muslim countries also led to the incursion of a value system that was alien to the mission and message of Islam. In the aftermath of the West's dominant influence, the Muslim countries suffered a major inferiority complex that affect their corporate identity as a strong, unified ummah.

A timeless message embedded in the Qur'ān and the sunnah, Islam emerged from an environment that was cut off from the major civilisations like the Persian and Roman civilisation, noted for their high culture and military power. Arabia did not possess any refined accomplishments or civilisational contributions that it could boast of. On the contrary, the rugged life of its inhabitants and insularity from the civilised world did not expose them to any potential threat or conquest from these superior military powers.

The advent of Islam on the Arabian soil was an unprecedented event in the history of mankind. It heralded a new civilisation that was rooted in the divine laws revealed to the Holy Prophet (pbuh) that dealt a death blow to the corruptive influences which crept into the Persian and Roman civilisation. Islam conquered these superpowers of the day and brought about revolutionary changes that promoted the dignity of mankind and reasserted the universal values of equality and freedom. As a progressive, dynamic din it covered a philosophy of life that was based on Allah-awareness (taqwā) and accountability. Thus, there was no place for racial prejudice, religious bigotry and nepotism.

As a dynamic code of life Islam encompasses a value system from which flows norms and standards. Principles and thereafter laws follow in succession strengthening rules and regulations. In other words, the Islamic value system is organic, systematic and progressive in its vision and implementation. Sadly, when the ummah neglected the value system it became moribund, hidebound and retrogressive in presenting Islam as a civilisational force. Hence, it could not forge ahead as an ideological community towards salvaging humanity. The Holy Qur'ān categorically states that the ummah has been tasked to promote this value system that has the potential to eradicate the evils afflicting mankind. In sum, the *Khalifat Allah* envisioned by the Holy Qur'ān is only achievable by following the whole of Islam unconditionally.

Islam as an ideological community is endowed with salient features that take into account its da`wah-centric mission. Tawhid is positioned in all acts of worship (*`ibādāt*). Other faiths that can be regarded as ideological communities lack this all-embracing trait. Overall, their deviance from the originally revealed scripture accounts for this distortion. As a result, there is no prospects of these faiths carrying out this important responsibility.

There is a general tendency among Muslims to carry out their religious obligations as a routine. Salāh, for example, is performed without the spirit that should accompany it. Again, the elements of faith (*imān*) and introspection (*ihtisāb*) are not given any attention. This attitude betrays the real intent of the other pillars of Islam. In essence, there should be a balance between the external and internal forms of *`ibādah*. Likewise, the concept of the *shahādah* underscores the physical and spiritual dimensions of Islam. There are many incidents that relate to the spiritual masters (*mashā'ikh*) internalising in their lives the true content of faith.

Problem of Human Dignity

Human dignity as enshrined in the various *āyāt* of the Holy Qur'ān reinforces Islam's position on this universal principle. There is no contradiction in word and deed about the various facets of universal brotherhood that Islam advocates.

Islam preceded the Charter of Human Rights as adopted by the United Nations. Obviously, it was mandated and ratified by the member countries to give it an institutionalised form. In contrast, the fundamental rights of man with particular reference to human dignity was a core issue in the early years of Islam. Slavery as a lucrative trade existed in Makkah; moreover, many converts to Islam were slaves who were subjected to the worst form of punishment by their cruel masters. In the light of these humiliating situations, the Holy Qur'ān repeatedly reminded the believers of earning multiple rewards by freeing slaves from the shackles of oppression.

Human dignity in Islam is synonymous with the sanctity of life. In this instance freedom is equated with respect for individuals regardless of their racial background and their social position. The Qur'ānic phrase: "We have honoured the children of Adam" eradicates all distinctions of national and ethnic pride. Instead, it repeatedly reminds mankind about the benchmark of Allah-awareness (*taqwā*) in order to develop closeness to Allah.

There are numerous incidents contained in the *sirah* literature that illustrate the importance of human dignity. The Holy Prophet (pbuh) taught his illustrious Companions (Sahābah) that brotherhood implied deep respect, refined manners and decorum in their interaction with their peers and even no-Muslims. Tolerance was just not a virtue in theory or relegated to the margins of political thought. On the contrary, it was demonstrated by the Sahābah in their lives. If they faltered in any way, the Holy Prophet (pbuh) pointed out their shortcomings which were immediately rectified through remorse, forgiveness and reconciliation.

Another pertinent problem related to human dignity was the status of women. It is generally assumed that the deplorable position of women only existed in pre-Islamic Arabia. The *jāhilliyah* period (Days of Ignorance) associated with the Arabs is an instance in case.

Ancient Greece, for example, which made a huge impact in philosophical studies, fared no better in assigning a proper role for women. Debates about whether women possessed a soul, a bizarre statement, were meant to ridicule them. Essentially, there was no place of dignity for women in European religious thought.

Men and women in Islam were given equal status: there was no discrimination that marginalised women. In addition, Islam recognised their differentiated role in society compared to men according to the laws of nature. Their status was sanctified as mentioned in the hadith literature. Their right to inherit, for example, was a revolutionary step that raised their stature in society. Likewise, the Prophetic dictum of treating wives gently closed the doors of gender violence and fostered a culture of reverence, security and stability for them. In the same vein, "paradise (*jannah*) lies under the feet of a mother" reinforced in practical terms the dignity accorded to women.

The law of equity (*qisās*) in the broader sense meant justice and equality for all mankind. In other words, there were no privileges for the elites if they were found guilty of any offence. Nor could they flout the laws of the shari`ah with impunity. During the caliphate of Sayyidinā `Umar, he firmly applied these laws to ensure that there was no distinction between the governors and the people. Equality before the law ruled out the possibility of nepotism and likewise accountability strengthened the cause of human dignity.

Human dignity is entrenched in the Islamic code (shari`ah) and governs a believer's attitude, interaction and relationship with others. Qualities of mutual respect, compassion and selfless service permeate the collective life of a believer who seeks to please Allah at all times. He shuns egoism and arrogance and sacrifices his comfort for the sake for others. Humility and an all-embracing love for mankind are the hallmarks of his character. In the Holy Prophet's *uswah al-hasanah* there are sublime examples of human dignity. When the Holy Prophet (pbuh) announced that if he had hurt anyone then they should take redress. A person complained that the Holy Prophet's (pbuh) stick had scratched his body to which the Noble Messenger replied that he should do the same. The person pointed to the upper part of the Holy Prophet's (pbuh) back. He raised his shirt for the man who had another motive: to have the honour of kissing the blessed back of the Holy Prophet (pbuh).

As believers we should do some introspection: are our conduct a reflection of the ideals that were exemplified by the teachings of the Holy Prophet (pbuh)?

Why Religion

According to Islam, God is Unity. Then because God is Unity and He has created everything of this world, the world or this cosmos is Unity. This further means that this cosmos is a moral order and a reign of Law. Because God is Unity and this world is unity, there can be no such thing as sacred knowledge or profane (worldly knowledge). He has created the human individual but the individual personality cannot be conceived as composed of different facets and faculties placed in watertight compartments. Thus, the human individual will be conceived as an organic unity and the entire human pursuit in this life will have to be perceived in this fashion. (Simply put, there is unity in purpose in Islam because when a Muslim proclaims the Oneness of Allah (*tawhīd*), he also reinforces the oneness of mankind (*wahdat*).

Islam versus Communism

Islam stands definitely and positively for the purest form of tawhid and builds its entire philosophy on the belief in one God. Islam has given the proper place to social justice (which Communism does not advocate in the true sense). We are expected to be just even if it conflicts with our own interest and the interests of our family. We must be even just when dealing with our own worst enemy. Unless people are treated with justice, there can be no proper godliness in Islam for godliness is justice.

Islam was conscious of the fact that if basic needs are not fulfilled, then the higher values would be impossible to attain. Thus, the Holy Prophet (pbuh) proclaimed: "Poverty can lead to infidelity of God." (Communism is rooted in the exploitation of the masses in the name of equality and advancing its shambolic policies which aggravated their living conditions in an unequal society).

The Sunnah: The Challenge

Orthodoxy is a very holy word. What it means is that we should be true to the Qur'ān and the Holy Prophet (pbuh). But it has now taken the form of obscurantism (a trend to prevent enquiry, enlightenment and reform). Here in Islam, orthodoxy actually means dynamism. Some of the `ulama say they are orthodox but they are conservative. Orthodoxy is one thing and conservative is another thing. No community can actually survive in this world by being only conservative. There should be an amount of it for the sake of historical continuity only. But the world itself is not conservative. It is changing all the time. How can you be conservative and expect to survive?

Mawlud an-Nabi

The Holy Prophet (pbuh) is matchless. You cannot compare him to anyone of his creation. He is not a god, but he is the highest in Allah's creation. It is not something sectarian – it is the very foundation and spirit of Islam. Take it away and Islam is no more. Everything has a body and a spirit, and if the spirit is removed the body is dead. Take away the personality of the Holy Prophet (pbuh) from Islam and it becomes a lifeless ritual.

Is it human reason to accept that although Allah showers His praises on the Holy Prophet (pbuh) but made him no better than a piece of stone? Have we become so senseless because we are materialistic in our outlook? We are 'pygmies' and therefore we wish to measure the Holy Prophet (pbuh) with our 'dwarfish' status.

The Islamic Spiritual Quest

Islam gave a new approach, namely, the individualistic approach to life. You must be good morally, socially, intellectually, physically, individually and collectively. If you want to be good you must not indulge in all this sophistic paraphernalia of mysticism or ritualism. Don't you understand that during the last 500 years the Muslims have not made any immense contribution to human civilisation? What is the matter? Don't we feel ashamed? We are the founders of the modern scientific civilisation. We were the only superpower in the world for 1000 years. We were ahead of the entire world in war and peace, arts and science, philosophy, morals, spirituality, law and everything else. Where do we stand now? Why is Islam not helping us? It is because we are not taking help from Islam. It is useless talk only. If we use Islam as an opiate, it will actually shatter our nerves. Finally, if we use Islam as an elixir, it will revive us. So, Islam was used by the Holy Prophet (pbuh) as an elixir. We are not dealing with Islam in that manner at all.

HISTORIC LECTURES SERIES: AN OVERVIEW

The historic lecture series in South Africa by Dr Mawlānā Fazlur Rahman Ansari in 1970 and 1972 respectively are collated in the seminal work entitled *Islam to the Modern Mind*, which was first published in 1999. Essentially, the profound learning of Mawlānā Ansari in the classical Islamic *'ulum* (disciplines) and intellectual scholarship comes to the fore in these inspirational lectures. His writings ranging from philosophical works to his magnum opus, *The Qur'ānic Foundations and Structure of Muslim Society* bears the hallmark of extensive research, perceptive analysis and a brilliant mind.

Islam to the Modern Mind contains gems of Mawlānā Ansari's exemplary scholarship and concern for the ummah at large. It would be no exaggeration to state that this work represents the core message of Mawlānā Ansari's writings. It serves as an unbroken link to the *tabligh* vision that he embodied in his international *dini* travels.

The following lectures are contextualised to bring out their relevance to the writings of Mawlānā Ansari:

Muhammad the Prophet of Allah (pbuh)

As early as 1933 when Mawlānā was 19 years old he wrote *Muhammad the Glory of Ages* while a student at Aligarh Muslim University. The topics covered were: The age of *jāhilliyah*, advent of the Prophet (pbuh) and his call, Prophetic ideal and the Prophet's contribution to knowledge.

This was a celebrated book which was based on primary sources and the writings of Orientalists whom he rigorously critiqued. When Mawlānā Ansari wrote the two-volume *The Qur'ānic Foundations*, he expanded on the topics covered in *Muhammad the Glory of Ages*. In fact, the lectures dealing with the varied aspects of the Holy Prophet's life and mission in *Islam to the Modern Mind* resonate with multidimensional personality of the Holy Prophet (pbuh).

Love for the Holy Prophet (pbuh) in all facets of our life is not a formal attachment but should be a positive commitment in the following ways:

- To respect him above all created things;
- To love him above all created things;
- To obey him without demur (objection);
- To be absolutely loyal to him.

Mawlānā Ansari repeatedly makes mention of the Holy Prophet (pbuh) as the inaugurator of modern science, which is free from superstitious belief and bigotry. Here again Mawlānā Ansari reminds the Muslims that the 'new knowledge' that the Holy Qur'ān emphasised was based on a scientific outlook within a religious framework. In other words, the scientific quest with the right purpose and intention would be transformed into an act of worship (ʿibādāh).

Overall, it is act of total disrespect, Mawlānā Ansari argues for Muslims to engage in polemics and kufr-bashing to establish their love and attachment to the Holy Prophet (pbuh). Sectarian bickering and theological disputations are streaks of bloated egos that seek to establish a superficial relationship with the personality of the Holy Prophet (pbuh).

What is Islam

This lecture must be read with the *Principle of Tawhīd* to understand Mawlānā's presentation of Islamic beliefs and practices. The ideal religious life according to Ansari is to cultivate an unconditional faith in the meaning, message and teachings of the Qur'ān and the sunnah. Islam as a way of life (*din*) is comprehensive, dynamic and progressive. Unlike other religions (Hinduism, for example), it condemns the worship of deities and cluttered rituals that have no bearing to the concept of *tawhīd* (Oneness of Allah). Therefore, it is unthinkable for a believer to indulge in ceremonies that in essence and spirit contradict tawhid. This is a clear-cut violation of the Divine law.

In *What is Islam*, unity in a broader sense involves values that reinforce the spirit of brotherhood, self-sacrifice, mutual understanding etc. In What is Islam, Mawlānā Ansari provides an A-Z guideline of Islam as religion. As a dynamic, revolutionary religion it encompasses values that have directly influenced human civilisation. It is a religion of the highest idealism in ethics: submission to the Will of Allah (Islam) and internalising the Divine attributes in one's life.

Islam gives a practical demonstration of brotherhood in the exemplary conduct (*uswah al-hasanah*) of the Holy Prophet (pbuh) and his illustrious Companions (Sahābah). Therefore, adherence to the Prophetic teachings is a sublime act of obedience: it invokes a believer's responsibility of being the *Khalifat Allah* in all facets of human endeavours. Mawlānā Ansari explains: "Allah, the One, has created them all; and He originated the existence of the human species on the earth through one original pair of man and womankind. This gives us the Qur'ānic principle of the *Unity* of mankind, in which all prejudices of race, colour, caste and sex are obliterated and the only principle of distinction in respect of status is *achievement* in terms of spiritual and moral character and knowledge. As regards respect for human dignity, it is, in the Qur'ānic view, the birthright of every human being.

The Inner Dimensions of the Sunnah

Mawlānā Ansari makes a perceptive comment: The sunnah is an outward manifestation of inner quality. The inner quality as given in the Holy Qur'ān is *taqwā*." The basis of sunnah-centred life is the transformation of the heart (*tazkiyah*); all human values reached their perfection and refinement in the personality of the Holy Prophet (pbuh).

In *The Qur'ānic Foundations* Mawlānā Ansari elucidates fifteen facets of the sunnah encompassing the personality of the Holy Prophet (pbuh). These include spending every moment of life productively, gentleness and consideration for others, practice of mercy in all situations, extreme humility tempered with dignity, and promoting truth in every circumstance. At the same time, Mawlānā Ansari laments at Muslim narrow definition of the sunnah which deals with "too much fuss as to juristic (*fiqh*-related) hair-splitting" among the so-called orthodox pursuers of religiosity. This is a recurrent theme in his lectures about disproportionate emphasis on ward appearance of the sunnah. Against this rigid interpretation of the sunnah, Muslims need to internalise the spirit and culture of this primary source of Islamic teachings.

Salāh (Devotional Prayer)

Mawlānā Ansari emphasises the importance as demonstrated by the Holy Prophet (pbuh). It requires focus of the mind body and soul together with the synergy of humility and deep reverence of being in the presence of Allah. Salāh performed in the fashion of gymnastics takes away the communion between the `abd (servant) and Allah. Every gesture represents an act of humility, reaffirming our submission to Allah. Therefore, a distracted mind which is cluttered with otherworldliness serves no purpose in cultivating the essence of salāh.

Islam: An Introduction gives a detailed discussion on the philosophy of salāh. Mawlānā Ansari draws a beautiful comparison of salāh to maintaining a healthy diet. He lists three pre-requisites that are essential for strong and healthy body and then compares these to the essentials of salāh. Regarding the prescribed five obligatory (*fard*) prayers, Mawlānā Ansari states that feeding the soul should be regular and consistent through appropriate times. For example: "There comes a time in our physical stamina at noon when we have to replenish our energy by having lunch. Islam prescribes that we should revitalise on that occasion our spiritual energy by offering the *Dhuhr* (midday) salāh. The harmonious blending of the mind, body and soul is emphasised through the institution of the prescribed obligatory prayers.

Why Religion

This enlightening lecture delivered in the University of Cape Town held the audience spellbound. Mawlānā Ansari presented a logical, philosophical approach about the existence of God, the fusion of faith and reason in the religious quest, and more importantly, the creation of the universe with a definite purpose. In the question answer session that followed, Mawlānā Ansari employed philosophical terms to answer the complex questions about the fallacy of rejecting the existence of God. Likewise, life is not static and human beings are prone to different challenges in their daily lives. Mawlānā Ansari asks a rhetorical question: Is the world created by a chance order? To this he gives a befitting reply: "The worth in life and meaning in life comes only through believing in God and we should believe in God. Almighty for our safety, security and happiness."

In *Foundations of Faith* Mawlānā Ansari critically examines the function of religion by presenting compelling arguments on the fallacy of rejecting the rejecting God and His creation of the universe. For Mawlānā Ansari Islam present a simple, unsophisticated exposition of the creation of the universe by focusing on revelation (*wahy*) and the comprehensive message and teachings brought by the final Messenger of Allah (pbuh). So too is belief in the Afterlife which has a definite purpose in the scale of obedience in the light of the Qur'ānic teachings and the sunnah. For Muslims, heaven (jannah) in Mawlānā Ansari's *Beyond Death* " affirms the highest yearning of the realisation of the soul – vision of, and the proximity of Allah" as described in several verses (āyāt) of the Holy Qur'ān and the hadith literature.

Islam versus Communism

In the same strain of his perceptive lecture on *Why Religion*, Mawlānā Ansari presented a brilliant exposition on the ideological differences between Islam and Communism in the University of Stellenbosch. For Ansari, Communism thrives on expediency by making bold claims of serving the needs of the poor and establishing a society of classless people. Furthermore, Communism in reality believes in the dictatorship of a select few who are responsible for exploiting the masses through slavery and other forms of oppression.

Islamic values are rooted in self-sacrificing service and creating a just social order. In this way the moral and spiritual values are kept intact. During the caliphate of Sayyidinā `Umar, the social welfare department was perfected to ensure that every person, regardless of his religious background who lived in the Islamic Empire received his basic needs honourably.

Mawlānā Ansari had made an extensive study of Communism by documenting its history and aggressive that directly affected Muslim nations who had maintained their Islamic identity over the centuries. His critical examination of this atheistic system in *Communist Challenge to Islam* written on the 1940's is a testament to his rigorous scholarship. Mawlānā Ansari critically examines the so-called success of the Communist rise to power in the background of the Czarist regime that was in tatters. Communism employed the tools of propaganda in the name of social welfare and other slogans to create the illusion of a prosperous society without religion. In the same strain, Mawlānā Ansari provides a graphic account of the suffering of Muslim nation under the Communist regime and also highlighting a modernist group of Muslims embraced and promoted this ideology. It was not surprising therefore to see Muslim women discarding the purdah while these modernist intellectuals writing books with an anti-Islam bias.

Tasawwuf: Spiritual Pursuit in Islam

This lecture together with *Discipline in Dhikr* touches on the inner dimensions of *tasawwuf* in the light of the Holy Qur'ān and the *uswah al-hasanah*. Mawlānā Ansari emphasises an important point: *tasawwuf* devoid of the shari`ah is misguidance. By the same token, he laments the fact that a group of scholars who are fixated on the literal interpretation of the Islamic teachings are averse to *tasawwuf*. In the light of Islamic history, illustrious scholars belonged to the `alim-shaykh tradition and made immense contributions through *tazkiyah* to reform the   Muslim society in different eras and social milieus.

In a chapter devoted to *tasawwuf* and mysticism Mawlānā Ansari is critical of pseudo-sufis who have distorted the reputation of this illustrious tradition. In many instances, they have misinterpreted *tasawwuf* through the lens of mysticism, which is a violation of the inner dimensions of Islam. In Mawlānā Ansari's estimation, the transformation of the human personality is the heart (*qalb*). Moral virtues like truth, justice and beauty are triggers of transformation that activate the human personality to tread the path of *taqwā*. Likewise, attachment to a spiritual guide is a natural instinct, who guides a murid (aspirant) to reach the goals of *ihsān* (refinement and spiritual excellence).

The two-volume *The Qur'ānic Foundations* is a pioneering work in Qur'ānic studies and has been widely acclaimed for its comprehensive presentation of morality from the Islamic perspective. The themes explored in *Islam to the Modern Mind* are succinctly discussed in Mawlānā Ansari's magisterial work.

Conclusion

Gems from the Lectures of Mawlānā Ansari

- Muslims, take care before Islam becomes a memory of the past. Until and unless we organise education according to the Islamic concept, and produce God-fearing, morally integrated, spiritually elevated, intellectually enlightened Muslims in this community, we will have no future.

o Most Muslims are considered to be practising Muslims but tend to regard Islam as a cult, and not a comprehensive way of life. According to us it (Islam) is constituted of certain rituals and ceremonials, and hair-splitting about *aqā'id* (beliefs) is where it ends. We do not consider the moral value of life because we have divorced religion from morality. Observe how far our devotional piety is removed from our morality.

o Life is just a series of fleeting shadows – dreams – and nothing beyond that. We are sleeping here and will wake up when we die, for in our sleep we are seeing a continuous dream. This is *hayāt al-dunyā* (life in this world) and this is what our great *imāms* taught us. The term of life that we possess is about which none of us know when it is going to end.

o Those who walk on the earth in a light step are those who are grateful to Allah and to man, and have goodwill towards all. It is also those who behave like the refreshing morning breeze causing the buds to smile into flowers, bringing fragrance, vigour, happiness, and peace to human beings. This is the role of the Muslim.

o Let us take the example of charcoal. We know that charcoal is pure carbon and diamond is pure carbon. It is only the frequency of the vibration of the molecules that makes them different. The Holy Prophet (pbuh) is a human being. We are human beings too but he is like a diamond and we are like charcoal! Would anyone like to exchange his diamond for a hundred bags of charcoal? There is a world of difference between the worth and value of the two.

o Once the inner values (of the sunnah) have been built, then it becomes an obligation of love that a person's inner-self becomes an image of the Holy Prophet's (pbuh) personality. Naturally his outward form will also reflect the outer personality of the Holy Prophet (pbuh). But to try to build the outer only is like having a timber wall where the wood is infested with white ants. Painting is only done on the outside and not inside. Subsequently, the wood is being eaten by the white ants and as such the structure will not last.

o The Holy Prophet (pbuh) has laid down a law for us that our destiny is to become " imbued with Divine attributes" and for this we need to be magnetised. And how can we be magnetised? Unless the iron filings are within the range of the magnetic field, they will not be magnetised. The range has to be acquired by us by drawing nearness to Allah.

o When man becomes the *Khalifat Allah* he realises his potential status. In botany, every seed contains the plant that grows out of it, potentially. Similarly, every human being is *Khalifat Allah* potentially. He or she has to develop himself or herself in accordance with that code of Islamic guidance to become *Khalifat Allah*. From this perspective, Islam is a treasure house of the blessings of Allah. We can benefit from this inexhaustible treasure house only if we follow the model of our beloved Prophet (pbuh), love him intensely and to become like him in nature – actually.

o Every Muslim should study Islam and the Qur'ān. Study the message. Let us investigate for ourselves and we will find that Islam today is the only panacea for the ills and problems of mankind. Islam is the alchemy that can turn base metals into gold. Islam can benefit us in this world and the Hereafter. In this way, the seeker will acquire real imān. Islam did not come to wage war, but to advise positive living, to invite others with love and affection, with sympathy and the best of goodwill.

o Therefore, why should we believe in God? If I am here by chance, the world is a chance order. Life then is just a blind process and has no meaning. Is life worth all this? It cannot be. The worth in life and the meaning in life comes only through believing in God and we should believe in God Almighty for our safety, security and happiness.

o And if our ideal is to establish those ideals (as outlined in several verse of the Holy Qur'ān) the work of practising Islam in its entirety) can be done methodically, like in a scientific analysis. Prioritise one value after the other. If we do that, we will get an Islam that is very dynamic, progressive and enlightened. There will be no difficulty in living here as good Muslims and we will be able to live Islam in a manner that will attract the non-Muslims.

o   Your obligation is to be just in your dealings with people. This is the principle of justice that supports unity. Why does disunity come into the community? If you analyse the problem you will find that disunity comes through the clash of egos. When the individual egos are projected, justice cannot be satisfied. The very name Islam means "annihilation of the ego" or "submergence of the ego" into the Divine pleasure (rida ilāhi). It starts from this point and then gives the principle of justice in clear terms.

o   Turn back to that source of life (Qur'ān and the sunnah). And Inshā-Allah, this small community in South Africa will be a beacon of light and provide guidance to other communities. Our function is to be a beacon of light towards a higher life: godliness, absolute justice, truth, beauty, wisdom and holiness. We have to become this! We have the resources in the community; we only need to rediscover ourselves as to *what* we are and *what* we ought to become.

o   Another principle of priority is that the individual cannot live in a vacuum. Every individual is always part of a larger group. For example, one is part of a family, then the community, then the town, city or country. In fact, one is part of the entire human family and finally, part of the universe. So, if a human being does not have a social perspective and builds himself as a socially being in the way the Qur'ān and hadith advocates, he may be a failure. Thus, all these dimensions have to be taken into consideration. To observe the obligatory rituals of praying, fasting and charity must be done, but remember, life is a unity.

o   My dear sisters, beware of the ghost of modernism, of vulgarity, obscenity and shameless behaviour. That destroyer of the purity and dignity of womanhood is invading the homes of your country. The bacteria of this plague are here and spreading fast. If you wish to save your dignity and preserve the values of human life, you will have to take a definite stand against all this. I know that Muslim communities are tossing and turning between the evils of modernism and conservatism. I am sure most of you are educated and possess a sense of what is good and what is bad. I therefore appeal to all mothers, daughters and sisters to stand up and wage an all-out war against this devil of destruction which is in your midst and appears with an innocent face but with a dagger concealed. May Allah protect you all.

o The practice of *tasawwuf* in the Muslim world has degenerated and it is very difficult to find it in its original form as it was given. I know how this noblest of pursuit has been commercialised, ritualised and degraded by many a person who claims to be a spiritual guide (murshid) of a certain order. All this is due ignorance on the part of the general Muslims and those who represent this noble pursuit. In contrast, *tasawwuf* is nothing else but the effort to fulfil that mission of the Holy Prophet (pbuh) mention in the Holy Qur'ān as *tazkiyah* (purification of the soul) and in the hadith as al-ihsān (spiritual refinement and the beautification of Islam).

o Is it human reason to accept that although Allah showers His praises on the Holy Prophet (pbuh) but made him no better than a piece of stone! Have we become so senseless because we are materialistic in our outlook? We are 'pygmies' and therefore we wish to measure the Holy Prophet (pbuh) with our dwarfish status. Remember, the measure of all things in this universe is only the Holy Prophet (pbuh).

o Understand your mission first of all as a human being. What ought to be our mission? Islam has not come to dehumanise us but to humanise us. We are by nature good, and we ought to be good Muslims. The conscious Muslim never stayed in a vacuum. Sadly, we have fallen behind in every branch of human activity. We used to teach others at that time, and these are now masters (on account of their advancement in science and technology).

o The message is clear: stick to the *Kitāb* (Qur'ān) and the sunnah!

www.ingramcontent.com/pod-product-compliance
Lightning Source LLC
Chambersburg PA
CBHW061305120726
48001CB00001B/494